SUPER SCIENCE EXPERIMENTS

Chris Oxlade

Consultant: John Farndon

Miles Kelly

First published in 2011 by Miles Kelly Publishing Ltd
Harding's Barn, Bardfield End Green, Thaxted, Essex, CM6 3PX, UK

Copyright © Miles Kelly Publishing Ltd 2011

This edition printed in 2017

4 6 8 10 9 7 5 3

Publishing Director Belinda Gallagher
Creative Director Jo Cowan
Editors Amanda Askew, Sarah Parkin, Claire Philip
Editorial Assistant Lauren White
Designers Joe Jones, Kayleigh Allen
Cover Designer Simon Lee
Photographers Simon Pask, Alex Bibby
Production Elizabeth Collins, Caroline Kelly
Reprographics Stephan Davis, Thom Allaway,
Anthony Cambray, Jennifer Cozens, Lorraine King
Assets Lorraine King

ISBN 978-1-78209-423-4

Printed in China

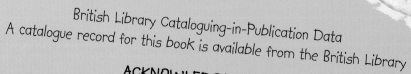

British Library Cataloguing-in-Publication Data
A catalogue record for this book is available from the British Library

ACKNOWLEDGEMENTS
The publishers would like to thank the following sources for the use of their photographs:
Shutterstock.com COVER Ohn Mar; 6 sydeen; 7 Nir Levy, 29(br) Dmitry Yashkin, 50(tr)
Ivan Cholakov Gostock-dot-net, 73(tr) Sean Gladwell, (c) Brian A Jackson,
(br) travis manley, (bl) fatbob Fotolia.com COVER; 51(tr) Andres Rodriguez

Every effort has been made to acknowledge the source and
copyright holder of each picture. Miles Kelly Publishing apologises
for any unintentional errors or omissions.

Miles Kelly Publishing is not responsible for the accuracy or suitability of the
information on any website other than its own. We recommend that children are
supervised while on the Internet and that they do not use Internet chat rooms.

Made with paper from a sustainable forest

www.mileskelly.net

CONTENTS

Learn lots about science and how it works!

ELECTRICITY   6-27

AIR AND WATER   28-49

MATTER AND MATERIALS   72-93

LIGHT AND SOUND   50-71

Using this book

Each experiment has numbered instructions and clear explanations about your findings. Read through all the instructions before you start an experiment, and then follow them carefully, one at a time. If you are not sure what to do, ask an adult.

Experiment symbols

① Shows how long the experiment will take once you have collected all the equipment you need.

② Shows if you need to ask an adult to help you with the experiment.

③ Shows how easy or difficult the experiment is to do.

① 30 min ② No help needed ③ Hard

ELECTRIC bubble-maker

In this experiment you send electricity through water. The electricity breaks up the water, making tiny bubbles of gas.

Introduction
See what you will be learning about in each experiment.

You will need
- work surface
- thick card
- clean, empty jar
- 2 lead pencils, the same length
- pencil sharpener
- water
- 9V battery

Things you will need
You should be able to find the equipment around the house or from a supermarket. No special equipment is needed. Always ask before using materials from home.

(a) Cut a square of thick card about 2 cm wider than the opening of the jar.

(b) Sharpen both ends of the pencils. Then carefully push the pencils through the card, about 2 cm apart.

(c) Half fill the jar with water. Then place the c... top of the jar and slide the pencils up or d... that their ends are level and underwater.

Don't let th... pencils tou... the botto...

⚠ Safety
If there is a 'Help needed' symbol at the start of the experiment, you must ask an adult to help you.

The warning symbol also tells you to be careful when using knives or scissors, or matches. Always ask an adult for help.

92

Labels
Handy labels will provide you with useful tips and information to help your experiment run smoothly.

Stages
Numbers and letters guide you through the *stages* of each experiment.

Colour coding
Shows which section of the book you are in.

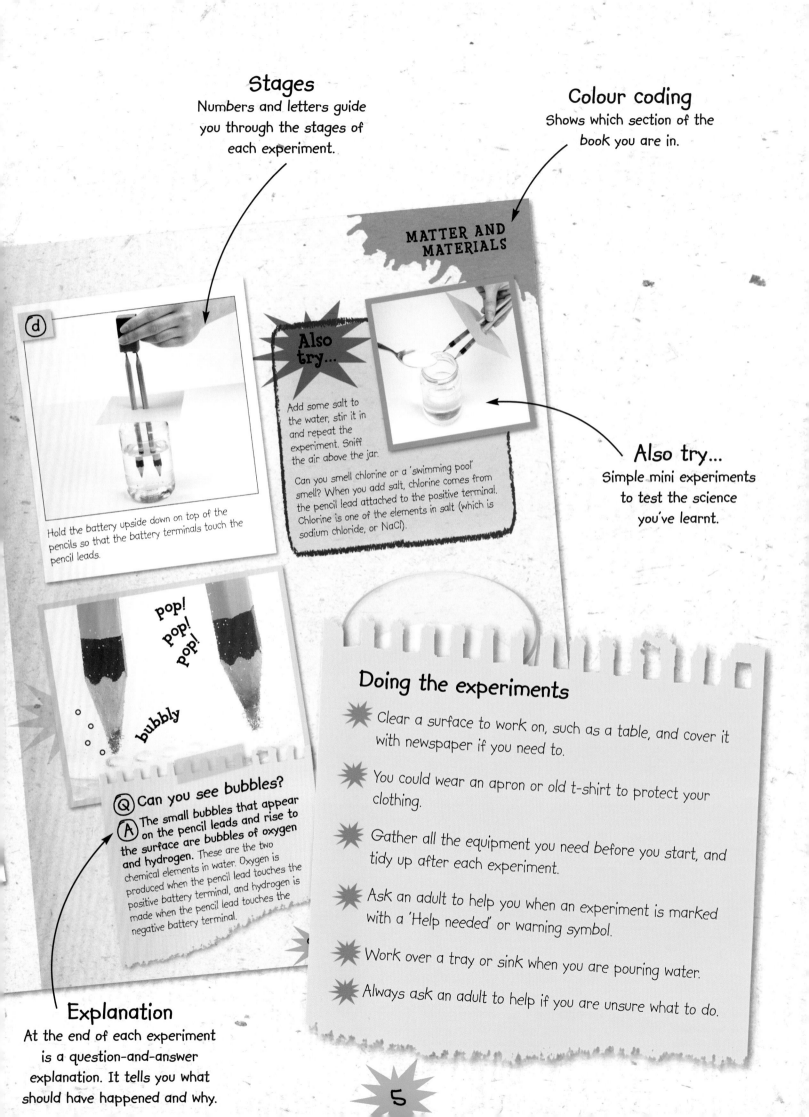

MATTER AND MATERIALS

d

Hold the battery upside down on top of the pencils so that the battery terminals touch the pencil leads.

Also try...
Add some salt to the water, stir it in and repeat the experiment. Sniff the air above the jar.

Can you smell chlorine or a 'swimming pool' smell? When you add salt, chlorine comes from the pencil lead attached to the positive terminal. Chlorine is one of the elements in salt (which is sodium chloride, or NaCl).

Also try...
Simple mini experiments to test the science you've learnt.

pop!
pop!
pop!

bubbly

Q Can you see bubbles?
A The small bubbles that appear on the pencil leads and rise to the surface are bubbles of oxygen and hydrogen. These are the two chemical elements in water. Oxygen is produced when the pencil lead touches the positive battery terminal, and hydrogen is made when the pencil lead touches the negative battery terminal.

Doing the experiments

✹ Clear a surface to work on, such as a table, and cover it with newspaper if you need to.

✹ You could wear an apron or old t-shirt to protect your clothing.

✹ Gather all the equipment you need before you start, and tidy up after each experiment.

✹ Ask an adult to help you when an experiment is marked with a 'Help needed' or warning symbol.

✹ Work over a tray or sink when you are pouring water.

✹ Always ask an adult to help if you are unsure what to do.

Explanation
At the end of each experiment is a question-and-answer explanation. It tells you what should have happened and why.

Electricity

What is ELECTRICITY?

Electricity is a kind of energy, and a major source of power for much of the world. It powers many of the machines we use every day. Electricity is produced in power stations, either by burning coal, oil or gas, or by using water or nuclear reactors to turn huge turbines.

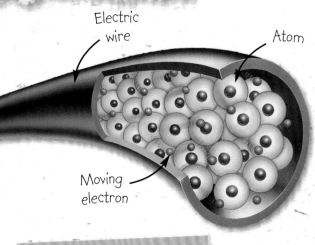

Electric wire

Atom

Moving electron

Creating a flow

Electricity as a power source depends on electrons, which are tiny parts of atoms. When electrons are pushed, they hop from one atom to the next. When billions of electrons are pushed, electricity flows. The push comes from a battery or a power station.

Materials

Conductors are substances through which electricity can flow. Metals such as copper conduct electricity well.

Insulators are materials, such as wood and plastic, that do not allow electricity to flow.

Electric circuits

An electric circuit is an unbroken loop of conducting material, along which electricity can flow. The three basic parts of an electric circuit are – an energy source such as a battery, a conductor and an object for the circuit to power, such as a light bulb.

An electric current flows through the copper conductor on the inside of the wire.

The outer covering is made of a plastic insulator, to stop electricity from escaping.

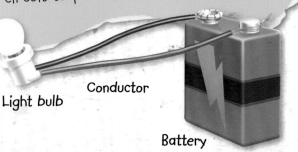

Light bulb

Conductor

Battery

6

Electricity in ACTION

Electricity is always at work around us – even when we can't see it! This is because all atoms can become electrically charged. Usually the balance between an atom's negatively charged electrons and positively charged centre is equal, but if the electrons are lost by being 'pushed', the object becomes positively charged. If electrons are gained, the object becomes negatively charged.

Static electricity

This is the build-up of electric charge on a surface. When you rub two materials together, electrons move from one object to the other – leaving one object positively charged and one negatively charged.

After a balloon is rubbed on hair, the hair stands up! Each strand has become positively charged, so they repel and move apart.

Attract or repel

Objects with opposite charges attract each other, and charges that are the same push each other apart (repel).

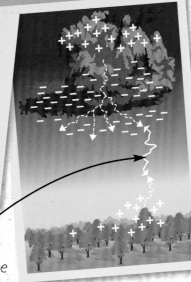

A negative charge from the cloud meets a positive charge from the ground.

Lightning spark

A lightning flash is a dramatic display of natural electricity. During a thunderstorm, a negative electrical charge builds up at the base of a cloud, while the ground has a positive charge. A lightning spark jumps between them to release the charge.

Magnetic force

Electricity is closely linked with magnetism – the invisible force between magnetic materials. When electricity moves, magnetism is created and when magnets move, electricity is created. Magnets are pieces of metal that can attract magnetic materials, such as iron.

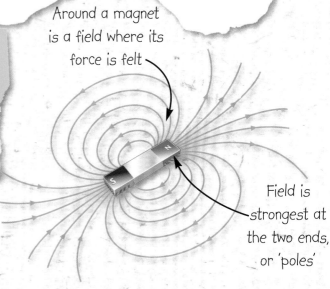

Around a magnet is a field where its force is felt

Field is strongest at the two ends, or 'poles'

ELECTRIC balloons

Does your hair sometimes stand on end when you brush or comb it? This is static electricity at work. When different materials rub against each other, electricity jumps from one material to the other.

30 min | Help needed | Easy

You will need

- work surface
- 3 balloons
- wool (sock or glove)
- small scraps of paper (such as tissue paper)
- metal spoon
- cotton thread, 1 m
- water
- scissors

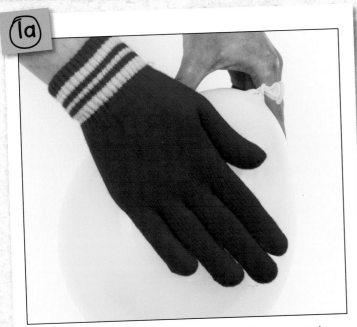

1a

Blow up a balloon and tie a knot in its neck. Rub the balloon with wool, such as a glove or sock.

1b

Cut the paper into small squares

Move the balloon over the small scraps of paper and watch what happens.

Also try...

Put a charged balloon next to your hair, or near a trickle of water from a tap and watch what happens.

Q Can a balloon pick up paper?

A Yes, when it has static electricity on its surface. Rubbing the balloon with wool creates a collection of electricity, called static electricity, on the surface. Tiny particles called electrons move from the wool to the balloon, giving the balloon a negative charge. This negative charge attracts positive electric charges in the paper. As the pieces of paper are small, the pull is big enough to pick them up.

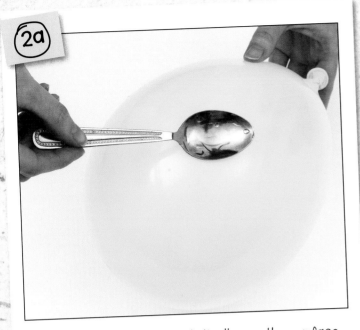

2a

Wet a metal spoon and rub it all over the surface of the balloon.

2b

Now test the effect of this by moving the balloon over the pieces of paper again. What happens this time?

Q Can you get rid of static electricity?

A Yes, rubbing the balloon with a wet spoon removes its charge. The static electricity on the balloon's surface flows away into the spoon (the water helps this happen by improving the metal's contact with the balloon). Now the balloon has no charge, so it can no longer attract the bits of paper.

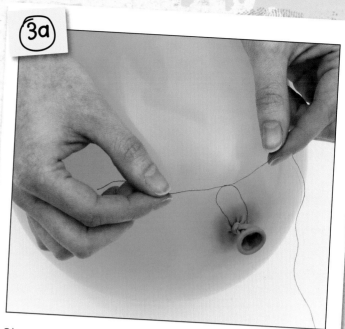

3a

Blow up two more balloons. Tie the end of the cotton thread to the neck of one of them, then rub both balloons all over with wool.

3b

Don't let the balloons touch each other

Ask a helper to hold the top of the length of thread, letting the balloon hang down. Move the other balloon towards it. Watch what happens to the hanging balloon.

Q Can balloons push each other?

A Yes, static electricity pushes the balloons apart. Rubbing the two balloons with wool creates static electricity on the surfaces of the balloons. The charges on both are negative. Charges that are the same (two positive or two negative) always push each other away (repel), so the balloons are pushed apart.

STATIC patterns

Some photocopiers and computer printers use static electricity to work. The static makes the marks you see on the finished page. Get ready to find out how this process works.

30 min · No help needed · Easy

You will need

- work surface
- plastic document wallet
- talcum powder
- sieve
- masking tape or plastic insulating tape
- plastic tray
- kitchen paper
- water
- scissors

a Shake some talcum powder through a sieve onto a plastic tray. The sieve helps to spread the talcum powder more evenly.

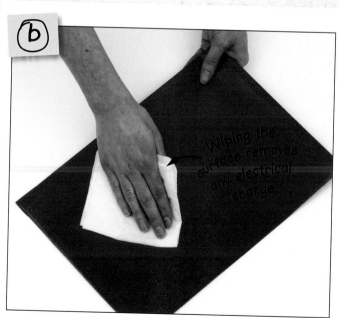

b Moisten a piece of kitchen paper with water and wipe it over both sides of your plastic document wallet. Then, dry the plastic thoroughly with a piece of kitchen paper. This will remove any static electricity from the surface of the plastic.

Wiping the surface removes any electrical charge

Cut pieces of tape and stick them onto the plastic to make a shape, such as a tick. Press the tape down firmly onto the plastic, but fold over the end to make it easy to rip off.

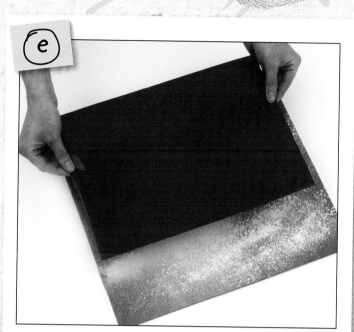

Turn the plastic over, but don't put it down. Very carefully hold it over the tray and lower it slowly, until it is just above the talcum powder.

Now you are ready to make your pattern. Put the plastic on a table and quickly rip off the pieces of tape.

Turn the plastic over to see what's happened.

Q Can I make a shape in talcum powder?

A **Yes, using static electricity.** Ripping the tape quickly off the plastic document wallet creates static electricity where the tape was stuck down. This happens because the tape and plastic are made from different materials. The electric charge attracts the tiny particles of talcum powder to the plastic, making your shape.

Simple electric CIRCUITS

A torch makes light using electricity. How does it work? This experiment shows how electricity flows round a loop to make the bulb light up.

15 min | No help needed | Easy

You will need

- work surface
- 1.5V AA battery
- short, thick elastic band
- scissors
- 3 lengths of kitchen foil, 20 cm x 2 cm
- 2 1.5V torch bulbs (not LED bulbs)

Preparation: Make a circuit

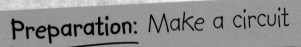

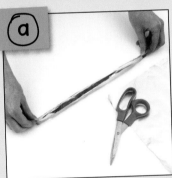

(a) Fold each of the pieces of foil in half twice, lengthways, to make thin strips of foil.

Put the small elastic band lengthways around the battery so that it goes over both metal terminals of the battery.

(b)

(c)

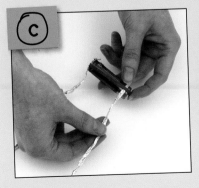

Put one end of each foil strip under the elastic band at each end of the battery. Make sure the two strips do not touch each other otherwise an electric current will flow.

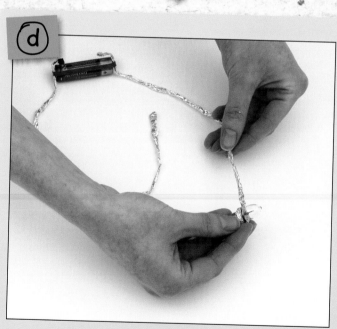

(d)

A torch bulb has two terminals (contacts). One is the metal casing below the base of the glass (the screw thread or bayonet prongs); the other is on the bottom. Wrap the end of one of the foil strips around the metal casing and twist it to make it stay in place. Make sure the strip does not touch the contact at bottom of the bulb.

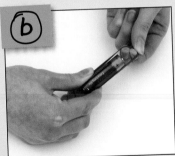

①

If the bulb slips out of the foil, hold the foil down with sticky tape.

Press the bottom contact of your bulb onto the other foil strip.

②a Wrap the second piece of foil around the metal casing of the second bulb.

②b Place the third piece of foil on your work surface.

②c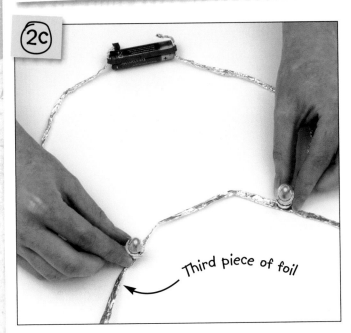

Third piece of foil

Put the bottom contacts of each bulb (which are connected to the battery with foil strips) onto the third piece of foil. What happens?

Ⓠ **How does a battery light a bulb?**

Ⓐ By connecting the bulb to the battery with the foil strips, you make a loop called a **circuit**. Electricity flows around the circuit. This flow is called an electric current. The battery is like a pump that pushes the current around the circuit. The current comes out of the terminal marked + (positive) and goes into the terminal marked − (negative). As the current goes through the bulb, it glows.

③

Wrap the second bulb in the same piece of foil as the first bulb

Take the foil strip with the bulb attached and wrap it around the side contact of the second bulb, further down. Press the bottom contacts of the bulbs against the other strip.

Ⓠ **Can you make the two bulbs glow brighter?**

Ⓐ Yes, by sending the electricity through both bulbs at the same time, not one after the other. We say that the bulbs are connected in 'parallel'.

Ⓠ **How can you light two bulbs?**

Ⓐ By putting the bulbs in 'series'. The electricity flows from the battery, through one bulb, then through the other bulb, and back to the battery. The light from the bulbs is quite dim.

CONDUCTORS
and insulators

Some materials let electricity pass through them easily. Others don't let electricity pass through them at all. Here's an experiment to find out which materials are which.

15 min   No help needed   Easy

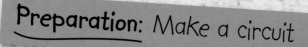
Preparation: Make a circuit

See page 16 for how to make your basic circuit. You'll only need two lengths of foil.

You will need

- 1.5V AA battery
- short, thick elastic band
- 1.5V torch bulb (not LED bulb)
- 2 lengths of kitchen foil, 20 cm × 2 cm
- scissors
- paper
- pen
- objects made from various materials, such as paper, wood, glass, plastic, metal

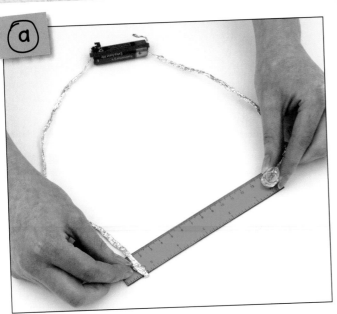

(a)

Touch the base of the bulb and the end of the second foil strip on either end of a plastic ruler or pen. What happens to the bulb?

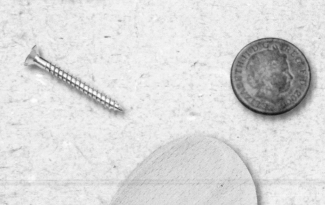

ⓑ Repeat step a using other objects. Each time, write down the name of the object and its material in a results table. Put an X next to it if the bulb does not light up, and a tick if it does.

OBJECT	MATERIAL	X ✓
Pen	Plastic	X
Ruler	Plastic	
Paper clip	Metal	
Book	Paper	
Pencil	Wood	

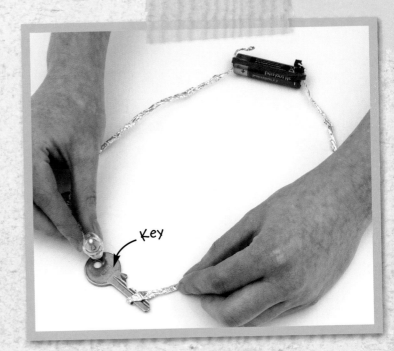

Key

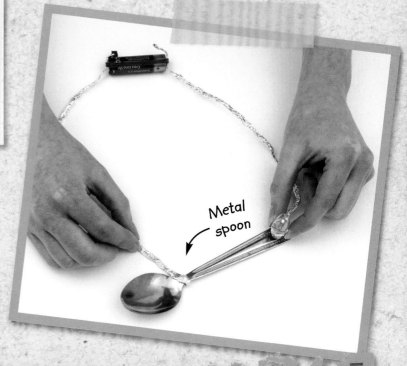

Metal spoon

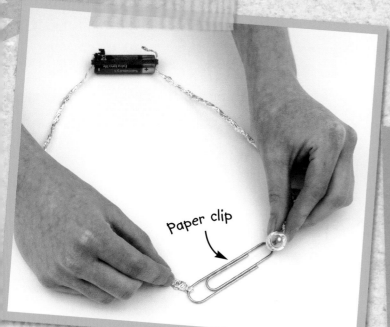

Paper clip

Q Which materials let electricity flow through them?

A Metals let electricity flow through them, lighting up the bulb. Metals are conductors. Other materials, including paper, wood and plastic, don't let electricity flow through them. They are insulators.

DETECTING electricity

How can we tell if electricity is flowing along a wire? You need a detector, such as a compass. A compass needle moves when it is near a wire with electricity flowing through it.

30 min | Help needed | Tricky

You will need

- 1.5V AA battery
- short, thick elastic band
- thin insulated electrical wire, 2 m
- 1.5V torch bulb (not LED bulb)
- sticky tack
- scissors
- 2 lengths of kitchen foil, 20 cm x 2 cm
- sticky tape
- wire strippers or a knife
- compass

Preparation: Make a circuit

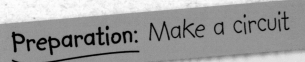

See page 16 for how to make your basic circuit. You'll only need two lengths of foil.

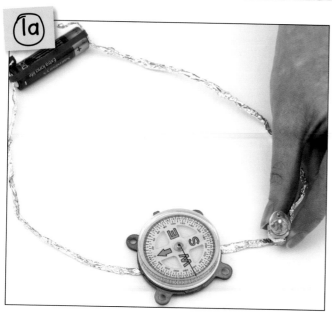

1a

Put the compass on top of one of the foil strips, then touch the strip with the bottom contact of the bulb. This completes the circuit and makes the bulb light up.

1b

Now remove the *bulb* to turn the light off. What happens to the compass needle?

(Q) Can you detect current?

(A) Yes, the compass needle detects the current. When electricity flows along the foil, it turns the foil into a weak magnet. This makes the compass needle, which is also a magnet, twitch.

Preparation: Strip some wire

Ask an adult to strip 2 cm of insulation from either end of the insulated electrical wire. This can be done with wire strippers or a sharp knife.

Preparation: Make a current detector

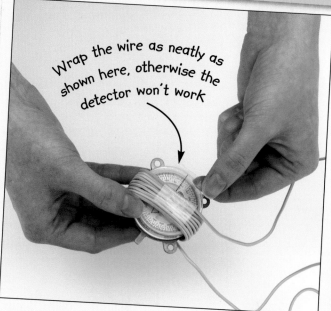

Wrap the wire as neatly as shown here, otherwise the detector won't work

Starting about 20 cm from one end of the wire, wrap the wire round your compass. Finish winding it about 20 cm from the other end. Use sticky tape and sticky tack to keep the wire in place.

(2)

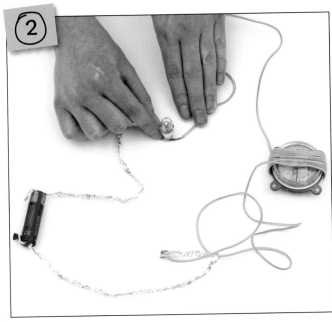

Attach one bare wire end to one of the foil strips, and the other end to the bottom contact of the bulb. Electricity will flow through the wire. Is the compass needle moving differently now?

Q Can I make the detector more sensitive?

A Yes, by wrapping wire around the compass. This turns the compass into a much stronger magnet when the circuit is complete and electricity is flowing through the wire. The stronger magnet makes the compass needle more sensitive to the flow of electricity.

Battery POWER

All sorts of electric gadgets need a battery to work. A battery is a source of electricity. Batteries make electricity from chemicals. In this experiment, you can see how this happens.

30 min   Help needed   Tricky

You will need

- copper coin or copper wire
- zinc-coated (galvanised) nail or screw
- table salt
- glass
- clothes peg
- sticky tape
- wire strippers or a knife
- jug
- water
- teaspoon
- 2 lengths of thin insulated electrical wire, 50 cm long
- I length of thin insulated electrical wire, 2 m long

Preparation: Strip some wire

See page 21 for how to strip wire. You'll need two pieces of wire about 50 cm long.

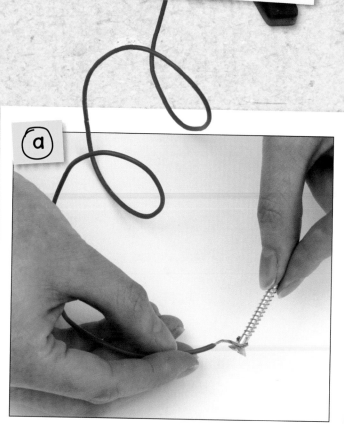

(a)

Wrap the stripped end of one of the wires tightly around the screw, just under the screw's head.

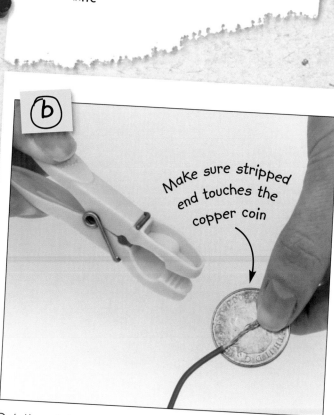

(b)

Make sure stripped end touches the copper coin

Put the stripped end of the second wire on top of the copper coin and hold it on using a clothes peg.

Preparation: Make a current detector

See page 21 for how to make a current detector.

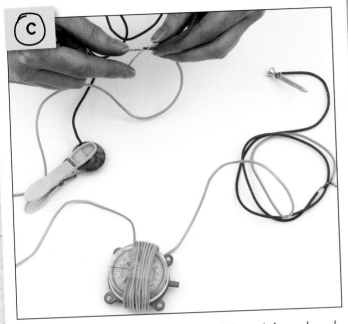

Twist together each of the remaining stripped ends of the two insulated wires to the ends of the current detector. Using sticky tape, attach the current detector to your work surface (to stop it moving around later).

Fill a glass with water and stir in a couple of teaspoons of table salt. Put the screw underwater in the glass.

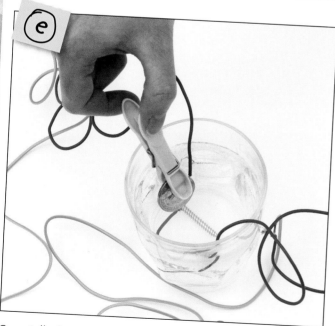

Carefully lower the coin into the water (don't let the coin touch the screw). As you do this, watch the needle on the current detector very closely. What happens? Take the peg out again – what happens?

Q Can coins and screws make electricity?

A Yes, by putting them in salty water.
The screw and the coin are made of two different metals (the screw is coated in zinc and the coin is copper). The water contains tiny particles with an electric charge. The different metals make the particles move through the water, and this makes an electric current – you should've seen the current detector twitch slightly as electricity was generated. Batteries work in a similar way.

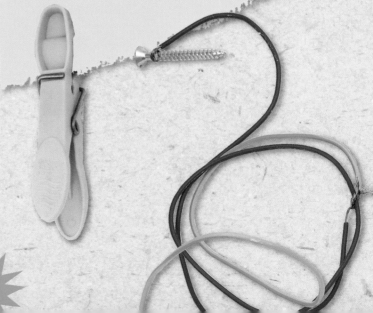

MAGIC magnet

This experiment shows that electricity can be used to make a magnet that will pick up small metal objects. The magnet can be switched on and off.

15 min Help needed Tricky

You will need

- work surface
- large steel nail (or screw)
- thin insulated electrical wire, 1 m
- 1.5V AA battery
- sticky tack
- paper clips
- sticky tape
- wire strippers or a knife
- short, thick elastic band

Preparation: Strip some wire

See page 21 for how to strip wire. You'll need two pieces of wire about one metre long.

Preparation: Make an electromagnet

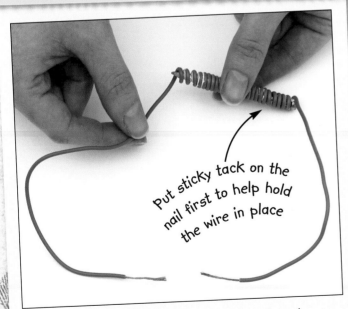

Put sticky tack on the nail first to help hold the wire in place

Starting about 10 cm from one end of the wire, wrap the wire tightly around the lenth of the nail up to the nail's head.

(a)

Put a small elastic band lengthways around the battery so that it goes over both metal terminals.

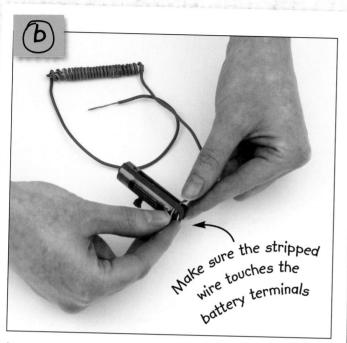

Make sure the stripped wire touches the battery terminals

Put each of the stripped ends of the wire from the electromagnet under the elastic band at each end of the battery.

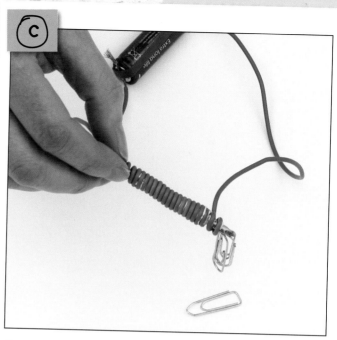

Put a few paper clips on the work surface. Hold the electromagnet with the pointy end of the nail close to the paper clips. Watch what happens to the paper clips. Don't leave the wire connected to the battery for more than a few seconds at a time, otherwise the battery will quickly run down and become hot.

(d)
After a few seconds, take one of the wires away from the battery. What happens to the paper clips now?

Q Can electricity pick up a paper clip?

A Yes, the electricity turns the nail or screw into an electromagnet. The electromagnet pulls on the paper clips because they are made of steel. When you take the wire away from the battery, the electricity stops flowing, so the electromagnet stops working and the paper clips fall back to the table.

Also try...

Make an electromagnet using twice as much wire. Adding another battery in series with the first, using another piece of foil to connect the two batteries end to end (make sure both are the same way round). Adding more wire and more batteries should make the electromagnet stronger. Can you pick up more paper clips now?

Buzz!
BUZZ!

Using an electromagnet, you can create a noise by making and breaking a circuit. This experiment shows you how to build a buzzer.

30 min   Help needed   Hard

Preparation: Make a circuit

See page 16 for how to make your basic circuit. You'll only need one piece of foil, and only follow stages a, b and c.

You will need

- work surface
- medium-sized metal paper clip
- sticky tape
- empty aluminium drinks can
- scissors
- 1.5V AA battery
- short, thick elastic band
- one length of kitchen foil, 20 cm x 2 cm
- large steel nail
- thin insulated electrical wire, 1 m
- wire strippers or a knife

Preparation: Make an electromagnet

See page 24 for how to make an electromagnet.

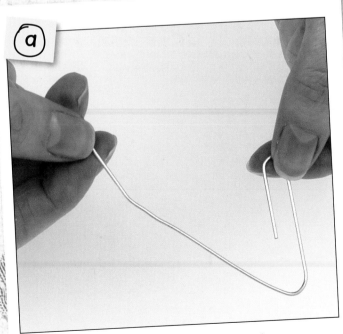

(a)

Straighten out the first two bends of the paper clip, so you have a straight piece of wire with a hook at one end.

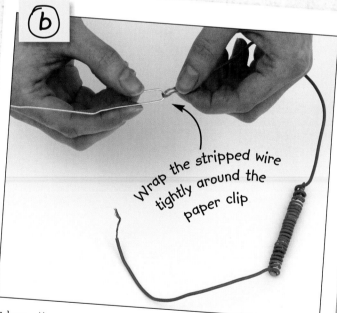

(b)

Wrap the stripped wire tightly around the paper clip

Wrap the end of one of the stripped wires from the electromagnet around the bend of the hook in the clip.

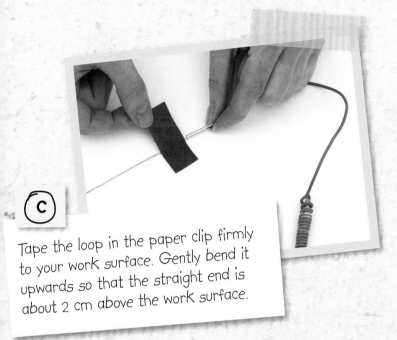

c

Tape the loop in the paper clip firmly to your work surface. Gently bend it upwards so that the straight end is about 2 cm above the work surface.

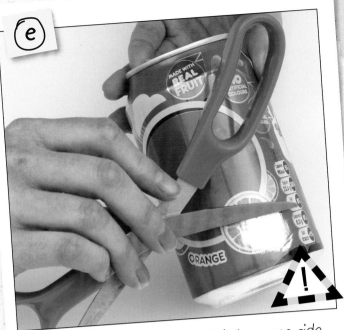

e

Ask an adult to scrape off the ink from one side of the can to make a patch of bare metal. Tape the spare end of the foil strip (attached to the battery) to the underside of the can.

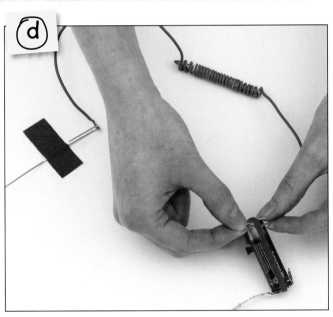

d

Put the spare stripped end of the electromagnet under the elastic band at one end of the battery, touching the terminal.

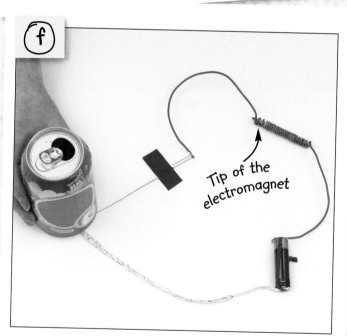

f

Tip of the electromagnet

Stand the can next to the straightened paper clip so that the end just touches the bare metal patch on the can.

Q Can an electromagnet make noise?

A Yes, by making a buzzer. The parts of the buzzer make an electric circuit. The electricity flows from the battery, through the can, along the paper clip, through the electromagnet and back to the battery. When the electromagnet is moved closer to the paper clip, it pulls the tip of the clip away from the can. This breaks the circuit, which turns off the electromagnet. As electricity stops flowing, the paper clip springs back to touch the can and reconnects the circuit. This happens again and again, making a buzzing noise.

g

Move the pointy end of the electromagnet slowly towards the centre of the straight part of the paper clip and listen carefully. What can you hear? If it doesn't work, adjust the distance between the electromagnet and the paper clip.

MAGIC moving wire

Some of the other experiments in this book showed how electricity can make magnets, and wires with electricity in them make magnets move. In this experiment, you can see how electricity and magnets can make a wire move.

30 min   Help needed   Hard

Preparation: Make a circuit

See page 16 for how to make your basic circuit. You'll only need two pieces of foil, and only follow stages a, b and c.

You will need

- work surface
- 1.5V AA battery
- 2 lengths of kitchen foil, 20 cm x 2 cm
- short, thick elastic band
- 3 lengths of copper wire, 1x 6 cm, 2x 12 cm
- bar magnet
- wire strippers, knife or pliers
- sticky tape
- scissors

a Tape the two long pieces of copper wire to your work surface, parallel to each other, about 4 cm apart.

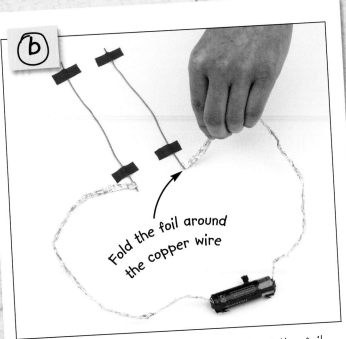

b Fold the foil around the copper wire

Take your circuit, and attach the ends of the foil strips to the copper wire.

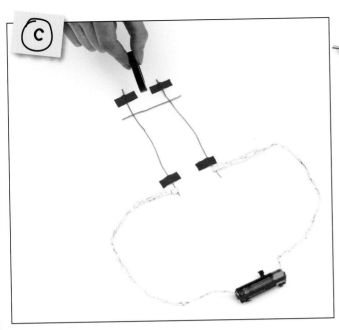

(c)

Put the shorter piece of copper wire across the two longer wires, completing the electric circuit. Hold one end of the magnet just above the centre of the shorter wire, and watch what happens. Don't leave the shorter wire in place for long as it will quickly make the battery run down.

Q Can a magnet move a copper wire?

A Yes, if a magnet is placed near a wire that has an electric current running through it. When electricity flows through the copper wire, it becomes a magnet itself. The bar magnet creates a magnetic field around the copper wire. This pushes the wire, so it rolls along. This is called the motor effect. All electric motors use this to work.

As the short piece of copper wire moves, the electric circuit stays intact

Also try...

Turn the magnet around so the opposite end is near the wire. The wire should move in the opposite direction to before because you are using the opposite pole of the magnet. Now try swapping the pieces of foil, so they touch opposite terminals on the battery. The wire should move the opposite way, too, because the electricity flows in the opposite direction through the wire.

Electricity with SALT

Some liquids let electricity flow through them. In this experiment you can see how electricity flows through salty water.

15 min   No help needed   Tricky

You will need

- work surface
- glass
- 1.5V AA battery
- short, thick elastic band
- table salt
- thin insulated electrical wire, 2 m
- 2 lengths of kitchen foil, 20 cm x 2 cm
- sticky tape
- wire strippers or a knife
- scissors
- compass
- water

Preparation: Make a circuit

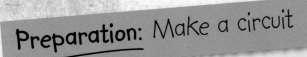

See page 16 for how to make your basic circuit. You'll only need one piece of foil, and only follow stages a, b and c.

Preparation: Make a current detector

See page 21 for how to make a current detector.

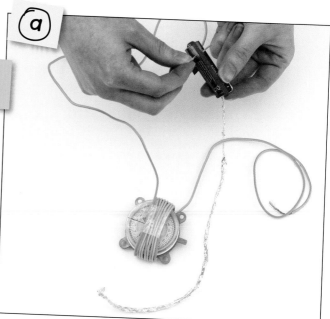

(a)

Put one of the stripped wire ends from the current detector under the elastic band at one end of the battery (attached to the foil strip on the circuit).

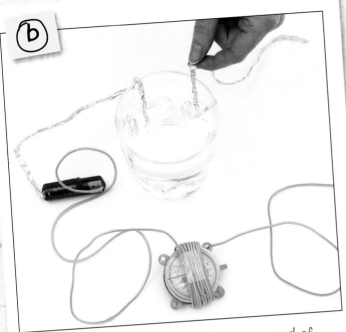

Fill the glass with water. Fold the spare end of the foil (attached to the battery) over the lip of the glass, so that the last few centimetres are in the water. In the same way, fold a spare strip of foil over the lip of the glass.

Add a teaspoon of salt to the water in the jar and gently stir it in. Repeat step c again. What happens this time?

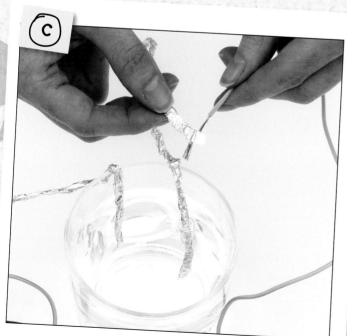

Attach the second strip of foil to the spare stripped end of the electricity detector. What happens to the compass needle?

Q Can salt make electricity flow?

A Yes, when you add salt to the water, more electricity flows. The compass needle in the current detector twitches if the wire touches the foil, because the circuit is complete. With plain water in the jar, only a tiny amount of electricity flows. When you add salt, the amount of electricity increases, so the needle twitches more. This happens because the salt breaks into tiny particles that are charged with electricity, which then carries the electricity through the water.

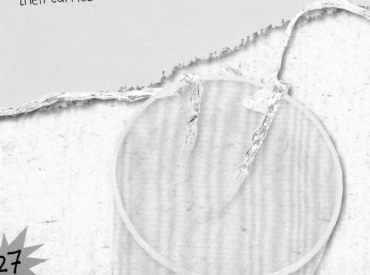

Air and Water

All about AIR!

You can't see it, but you can't live without it! Air is all around us, and it contains the oxygen we need in order to live. Air has weight, and it is pressing on you all the time, although you can't feel it.

Air pressure

Tiny particles in air, called molecules, are always bumping into each other. The more this happens, the greater the air pressure. The higher up you go, the lower the air pressure, and the less oxygen there is in the air.

In the air

The air consists of a mixture of gases, mainly nitrogen and oxygen, and also dust and moisture.

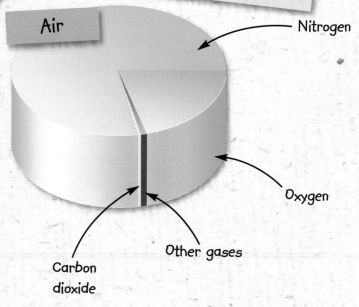

Air

Nitrogen

Oxygen

Other gases

Carbon dioxide

Atmosphere

Exosphere
500–800 km

Thermosphere
80–500 km

Mesosphere
50–80 km

Stratosphere
10–50 km

Troposphere
0–10 km

The atmosphere

Our planet is wrapped up in a blanket of air. We call this blanket of many layers the atmosphere. It stretches hundreds of kilometres above our heads. The atmosphere keeps in heat at night, and protects us from the Sun's rays during the day.

28

All about WATER!

All life depends on water – no animals or plants could survive without it. Most of the world's water is in the oceans and is salty. Fresh water, with no salt, is found in rivers and lakes.

Three forms of water

Water is the only substance that can exist as a solid (ice), a liquid (water) and a gas (steam) at normal temperatures. It melts at 0°C and boils at 100°C.

Water molecules

Water is made of two hydrogen atoms and one oxygen atom. It has a chemical formula of H_2O. A water molecule is shaped like the letter 'V'.

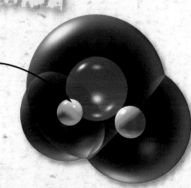

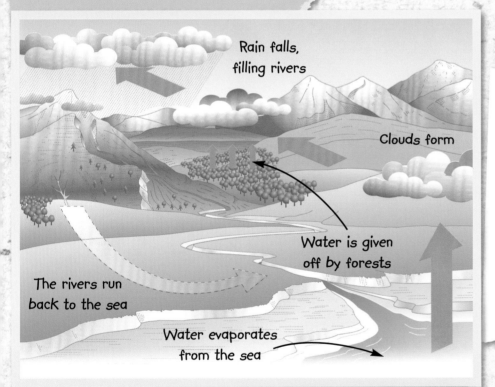

Rain falls, filling rivers

Clouds form

Water is given off by forests

The rivers run back to the sea

Water evaporates from the sea

The water cycle

All the water on Earth is involved in the water cycle. Water droplets or vapours rise from lakes, rivers and seas to form clouds. These droplets join to make bigger drops that eventually fall as rain. Much of the rain runs back into the sea.

Floating and sinking

When an object is placed in liquid, its weight displaces (pushes away) a volume of the liquid. This liquid pushes back on the solid with a force called 'upthrust'. If the upthrust is equal to or greater than the object's weight, the solid will float. An object will sink until its weight is equal to the upthrust of the water.

FLOAT
or sink

In these experiments, you see that some things float and some things sink. You can also see why materials that normally sink can be used to make boats that float.

You will need

- work surface
- washing-up bowl or sink
- balloon
- water
- small block of wood
- small bowl
- small plate
- modelling clay or sticky tack
- optional: food colouring

①

Push down

Fill the washing-up bowl with water. Blow up the balloon and tie a knot in it. Put the balloon in the water and push it under. Then let go.

Ⓠ Does the balloon float?

Ⓐ **Yes, when you push the balloon underwater and let go, the water pushes the balloon back up.** This is called the buoyant force. Water always pushes up on anything you put in it. The size of the force on an object depends on how much water the object pushes out of the way.

②

Put the piece of wood in the bowl of water. Push it underwater and then let go.

Ⓠ Does the wood float?

Ⓐ **Yes, the wood floats.** When it is underwater, the buoyant force on the wood is larger than its weight, so it floats to the surface.

30

③

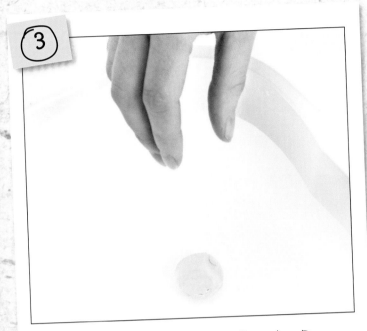

Roll a ball of sticky tack or modelling clay. Drop this in the water, too.

Ⓠ Does clay sink?

Ⓐ Yes, it sinks. This happens because the buoyant force on the ball of clay is less than its weight.

④ₐ

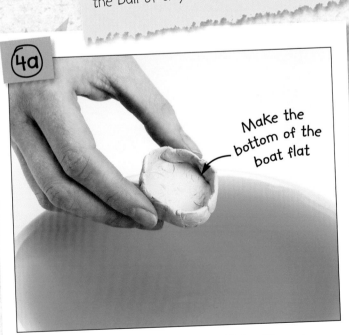

Make the bottom of the boat flat

Put a small bowl on a plate and fill it with water, right to the top. You could add food colouring so you can see the results clearly. Mould a piece of modelling clay into a boat shape and carefully lower it into the water.

④ᵦ

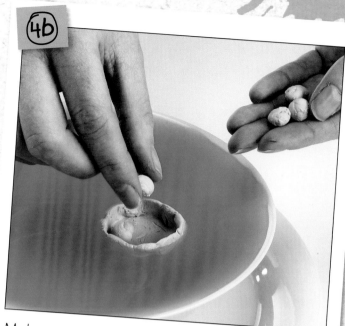

Make some small balls of modelling clay as cargo for your boat. Add them one at a time to the boat.

Ⓠ Does it sink?

Ⓐ Yes, eventually it will sink. At first, when you make the clay into a boat, its shape means that it pushes aside much more water than before, so it floats. As you load it up with cargo, it sinks down, so the buoyant force gets larger, balancing the extra weight. You can see that more water is pushed aside as some water overflows the top of the bowl.

Sunk!

Water overboard

FUN
fountains

Turn on the tap and water pours out. But it doesn't come out by itself – it gets pushed. The push is water pressure in the pipe. Here's an experiment that shows water pressure at work.

15 min   Help needed   Easy

You will need

- work surface
- large plastic drinks bottle
- craft knife
- ruler
- water
- jug
- marker pen
- washing-up bowl
- optional: food colouring

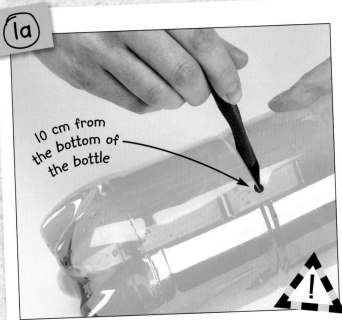

1a

10 cm from the bottom of the bottle

Remove the lid of a large plastic drinks bottle and draw a mark about 10 cm above the base. Using a craft knife, carefully cut a neat, round hole about 5 mm across. Ask an adult to help you.

1b

Fill a jug with coloured water (to help you see the water later). Stand the bottle in a washing-up bowl. Put your finger over the hole and fill the bottle to the top with the water. Then quickly take your finger away.

Q What happens to the water?

A The water shoots from the bottle. It is pushed out by the water pressure, which is caused by the weight of the water above the hole.

Whoosh!

2a

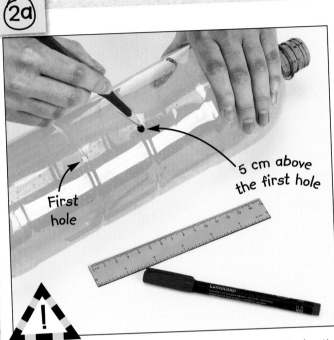

First hole

5 cm above the first hole

Carefully empty the bottle and cut another hole, the same size as the first, 5 cm above the first hole.

2b

Refill the bottle, again keeping your fingers over the holes to stop the water leaking out. Release both fingers at the same time.

Going...

going...

Q What happens?

A The bottom fountain is longer at first and then it quickly becomes shorter.

The pressure is made by the weight of the water pressing down from above the level of each hole. In deep water, the pressure is higher. The lower hole is deeper in the water, so the pressure is higher, making the fountain longer. As the water runs out of the holes, the water level falls, so the weight of the water above the holes reduces. The pressure at the holes drops, so the fountains gradually get shorter.

gone!

SKINNY water

You use water every day, but did you know that it has a skin? Here are some experiments to investigate how this skin works.

30 min | No help needed | Hard

You will need

- work surface
- shallow bowl
- paper clips
- water
- square of tissue paper (smaller than the bowl)
- washing-up liquid
- cotton buds
- clean, empty jar
- coins
- plate
- milk
- food colouring

1a

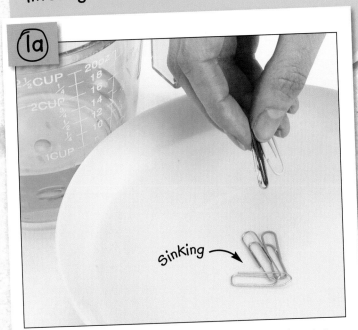

sinking →

Fill a bowl with water. Drop some paper clips into the water from just above the surface.

1b

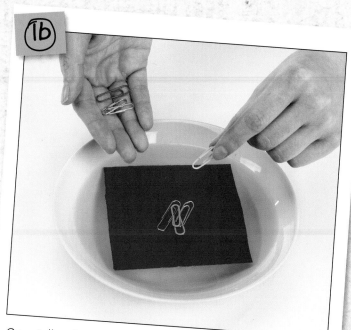

Carefully place the tissue paper onto the water's surface. Now place a few paper clips onto it.

1c

Put some of washing-up liquid on the cotton bud

Put some washing-up liquid on a cotton bud and touch the water's surface.

Q Do paper clips float?

A **No!** They are made of steel, which is heavier than water, so they sink. However, the surface of water can stop them from sinking because it acts like a skin. This is called surface tension where the water molecules at the surface are pulled towards each other. The tissue paper helps you to put the clips gently into the water so that surface tension can support them. Washing-up liquid breaks the surface tension, so the paper clips sink.

2

Put a plate underneath to catch spills

Fill a jar to the brim with coloured water (so you can see what's happening). Gently drop coins, one by one, into the water and watch what happens.

Q Does water bulge?

A Yes, the water surface gets gradually higher – until it is higher than the rim of the jar. Surface tension stops water overflowing from the top of the jar as you drop coins in.

Bulge!

3a

Fill a plate with milk. Carefully add a few drops of food colouring to the milk to make coloured spots.

3b

Dip a cotton bud into some washing-up liquid and touch the surface of the milk. What happens?

Q What does washing-up liquid do to the food colouring?

A It breaks surface tension in some places. Then the surface tension in other places pulls the food colouring into patterns.

Pretty patterns

Balloon SEESAW

Air is all around us, both indoors and outdoors. You can't feel it pressing down, so it's easy to think that it doesn't weigh anything. Try this experiment to show that it does.

15 min | Help needed | Tricky

You will need

- large space
- flat work surface
- long cane, about 1.5 m
- shorter cane, about 1 m
- 2 balloons
- duct tape
- sticky tape
- pin

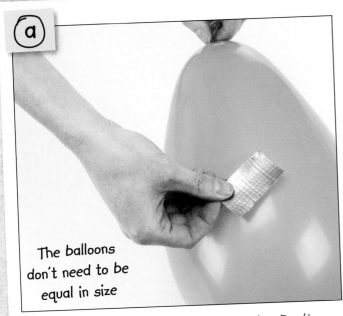

a

The balloons don't need to be equal in size

Blow up two balloons and tie their necks. Don't put in too much air or they will burst later. Cut a piece of duct tape about 5 cm long and stick it to one balloon.

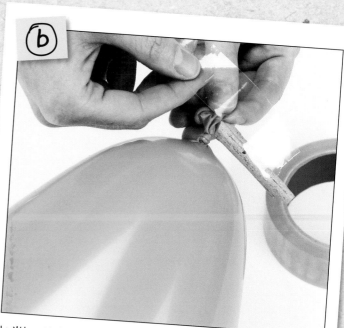

b

With sticky tape, attach the necks of the balloons to either end of the longer cane. The balloons should stick out at right angles, and both be on the same side of the cane.

36

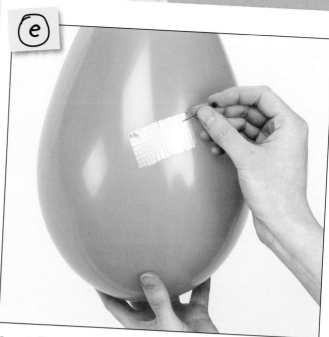

⒞ Fix the shorter cane to a flat work surface so it doesn't move, with at least 50 cm of it hanging over the edge. You could use sticky tape or heavy books. This cane will support the long cane.

Have patience! This is tricky

Rest the centre of the long cane on the short cane. Carefully move the long cane left and right, bit by bit, until it is balanced.

⒠ Carefully push a pin through the centre of the duct tape on the balloon to make a small hole. This will let air leak out slowly.

Ⓠ What happens as the balloon goes down?

Ⓐ **When you blow up the balloons, you squeeze air into them to stretch the elastic.** So each balloon is full of squashed air. With the cane perfectly balanced, there is the same weight on each side of the balance point. When you prick the balloon, air begins to escape. Very slowly, this balloon begins to rise and the other begins to fall. This means weight is being lost from the balloon. So the escaping air must have weight.

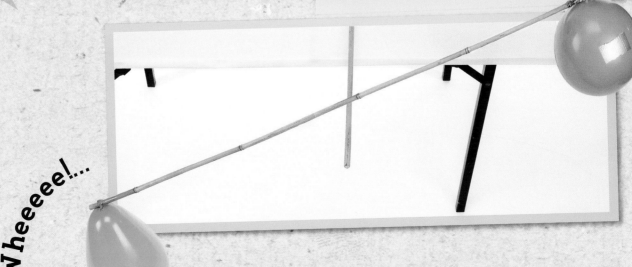

Wheeeee!...

37

ROCKET balloons

When air rushes out of a balloon, the balloon flies off. How far it flies partly depends on how much air comes out. Get ready for take off!

15 min   No help needed   Easy

You will need

- large space
- 2 chairs
- 2 long balloons
- 2 straws
- string
- sticky tape
- paper clips
- tape measure

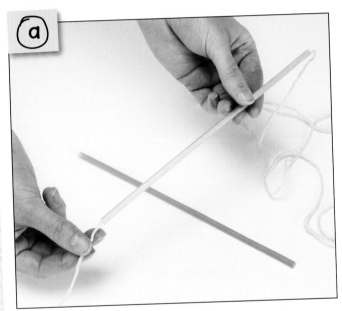

(a)

Cut two lengths of string, each about 5 metres long. Thread a straw onto each piece of string.

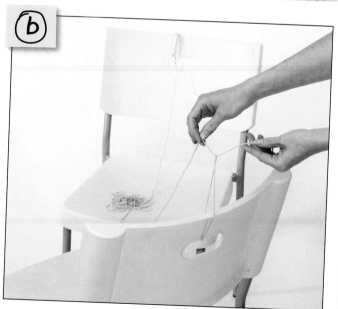

(b)

Tie or stick the string to the two chairs and pull the chairs apart so the string is taut. You'll need a large space to do this.

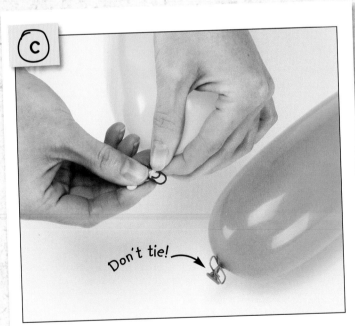

(c)

Don't tie!

Blow up one balloon completely, and the other balloon only half full of air. Twist the ends and attach a paper clip to stop the air from escaping.

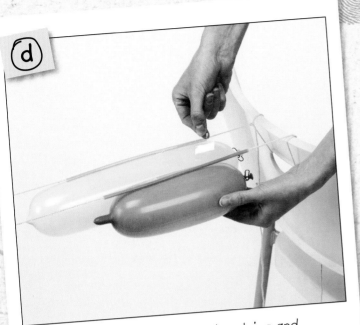

Pull the straws to one end of the string and attach the balloons using sticky tape.

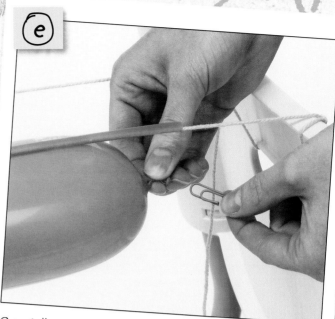

Carefully remove each paper clip. Make sure the neck of each balloon isn't sticking together. Let the balloons go and watch how far they travel.

Whooooooooooooosh! You can't catch me!

Q Which balloon travels the furthest?

A The balloon with the most air inside. The air inside a balloon is under pressure because the balloon is trying to squash it. When you remove the paper clips, the pressure pushes the air out. As the air comes out in one direction, it pushes the balloon in the opposite direction, just like a rocket. More air comes out of the bigger balloon, and at first is comes out faster. So the bigger balloon goes further.

The magic of AIR

Air is all around us and it also presses on us – with a push called air pressure. Get ready to see the amazing power of air pressure.

30 min   No help needed   Hard

You will need

- work surface
- 2 clean, empty jars
- washing-up bowl
- petroleum jelly
- square of thin card (bigger than the jar opening)
- optional: food colouring

1a

Fill a jar with water (make it coloured for fun). Smear the rim of the jar with a thick layer of petroleum jelly.

1b

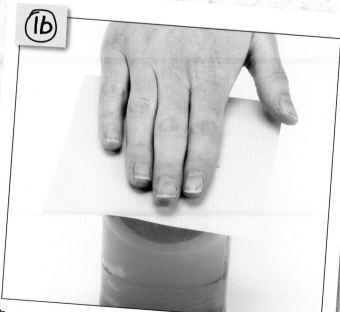

Put a square of card on the jar, so that it touches the rim all round.

1c

Hold the jar over a washing-up bowl, just in case

Support the card with one hand and turn the jar over. Take your hand away from the card.

Q Can card hold water?

A Yes, air pressure pushing up on the card keeps the water in the glass. This shows that air pressure pushes in all directions, not just down.

2a

Fill a bowl with coloured water (just for fun). Put the jar underwater so that it fills with water. Then stand the jar up so that the opening is underneath.

2b

Slowly lift the jar upwards out of the water. To begin with, the opening is underwater – what happens as you lift the jar more?

Q Does the water stay in?

A Yes, the water inside the jar should stay where it is instead of spilling out. It only spills out when the rim of the glass leaves the water. Air pressure pushes down on the water's surface. This pressure pushes the water up inside the jar.

¡Whoosh!

Also try...

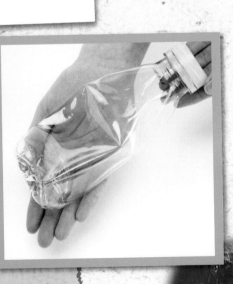

Pour warm water into a plastic drinks bottle until the bottle is about a third full. Swirl the water around the bottle a few times and pour it away. Put the top on the bottle and plunge it into cold water. The warm water heats the air inside the bottle. When you put the bottle in cold water, the air inside contracts, which reduces the air pressure inside the bottle, and the higher air pressure outside squashes the bottle.

Blowing TRICKS

This experiment demonstrates another property of air pressure – when air moves faster, its pressure goes down.

15 min

Help needed

Easy

You will need

- work surface
- small balloon
- large plastic drinks bottle
- card tube
- sandwich bag
- scissors

1a

Remove the cap of a large plastic drinks bottle. Using scissors, carefully cut off the bottom of the bottle.

1b

If the bottle gets wet with saliva, dry it

Blow up the balloon to the size of a ping-pong ball. Turn the top of the bottle upside down and drop the balloon into it. By blowing up into the bottle neck, try to blow the balloon out of the bottle.

Q Can you blow the balloon out?

A No, no matter how hard you blow! When you start blowing, the balloon is pushed up, but then the air from your lungs begins to flow under the balloon and around its sides. High-speed air has lower pressure than still air (this is called Bernoulli's principle). The pressure under the balloon falls, and the higher pressure air above the balloon pushes it down.

Wrap the bag tightly around the tube

Place a card tube into the opening of a sandwich bag and wrap the bag's neck around it (so that the tube is the only passage into the bag).

Now hold your mouth 10–20 cm away from the tube. Blow hard to make a narrow stream of air.

Try inflating the bag by putting your mouth against the end of the tube and blowing hard. Watch how the bag inflates.

Which bag inflates faster?

When you blow from far away the bag inflates faster. The fast-moving stream of air creates low pressure. This draws air in from around the entrance to the tube, which also goes into the bag, and it inflates faster.

Streamlined for SPEED

When you run, air pushes against you. This is called air resistance or drag. Air resistance pushes on anything that moves through the air. This experiment shows how.

 30 min

 Help needed

 Hard

You will need
- work surface
- 3 strips of thin card, 8 cm by 25 cm
- 3 squares of thick card, 10 cm by 10 cm
- sticky tape
- stapler
- hair dryer

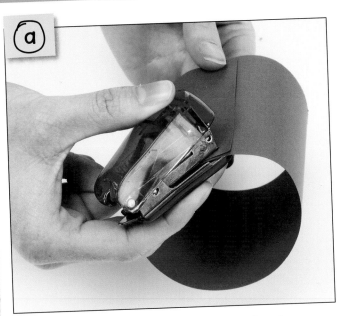

(a) Roll one of the strips of card into a tube shape. Secure with a staple at each end.

(b) *Make sure it keeps the circular shape*

Attach the tube to the centre of a square of thick card with two pieces of sticky tape, one on each side.

(c) Fold another strip of card into four equal pieces.

Stick the edges together with tape. Then fix the shape to a square of card with sticky tape.

The hair dryer should be level with your shapes

Stand the three tubes in line on a smooth table. Switch on a hair dryer and hold it about one metre away from the first shape. Slowly move the hair dryer towards the shape. At some point, the tube will begin to slide away. Try the same thing with the other two tubes.

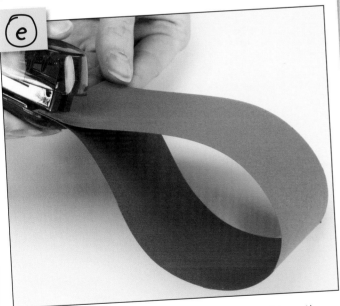

Press the ends of the third strip of card together to form a teardrop shape. Staple the ends of the card together and fix the shape to a square of card with sticky tape.

Q Which tube moves first?

A **The square tube moves first and the teardrop tube moves last.** Air flowing from the hair dryer hits the shapes, creating drag. The closer you move the hair dryer to the shapes, the faster air flows around them. And the faster the air flows, the greater the drag gets. Eventually drag becomes so great that it pushes the objects. The force of drag on an object depends on how easily air can flow around the object. The square creates the most drag and the teardrop the least. The teardrop is streamlined, allowing the air to flow smoothly around it.

FIRE extinguisher

Did you know that things cannot burn without air? But what happens to air when something does burn? Time to find out!

You will need

- work surface
- jug
- water
- matches
- small candle
- plate
- small, clean, empty jar
- large, clean, empty jar
- 3 coins, the same size
- modelling clay or sticky tack
- optional: food colouring

1a

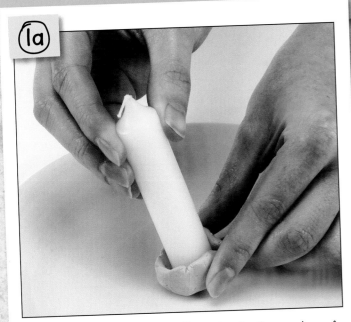

Put a small lump of modelling clay in the centre of a plate. Stick a candle into the clay so that it stands upright.

1b

The jar should be taller than the candle

Light the candle and place the small jar over it. Count how many seconds it takes for the flame to go out.

1c

Repeat the experiment again with a large jar. Does the candle burn longer this time?

Q Which burns better?

A A larger jar contains more air and so more oxygen, so the candle burns for longer. Air is a mixture of many different gases, but it is mostly nitrogen and oxygen. Oxygen is needed for burning. When you place the jar over a lit candle, the flame uses up oxygen. When the level of oxygen in the jar gets too low, the flame goes out.

Light the candle and put the jar over it, so that it rests on the coins.

Put three coins around the candle. They will support the rim of the jar.

Make sure there's equal space between each coin

Pour coloured water (so you can see what's happening) onto the plate until it covers the coins.

Q What happens to the water?

A The water level rises as the candle goes out. This isn't caused by the oxygen being used up, but by the air in the jar cooling and contracting when the flame goes out.

Model DIVER

In this experiment you use both water pressure and air pressure to make a model dive and surface.

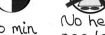

30 min | No help needed | Tricky

You will need

- work surface
- bendy straw
- paper clips
- large plastic drinks bottle with a lid
- glass
- scissors
- optional: food colouring

Preparation

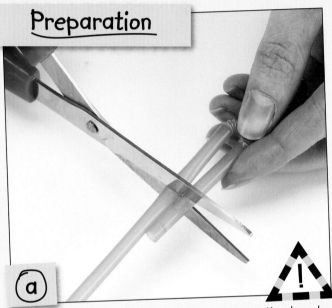

(a) Cut the straw about 2 cm either side of the bendy section.

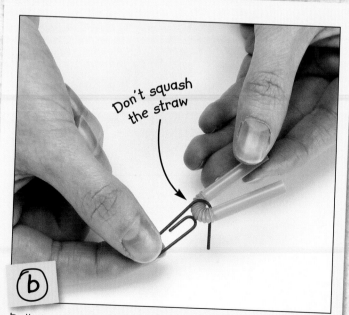

Don't squash the straw

(b) Pull the ends of the straw to extend the bendy section. Unbend the outer loop of a paper clip and wrap it around the straw bend. This is your model diver.

Test your diver

(a) Fill a glass with water to use as a testing tank. One at a time, add a paper clip to the bottom of the diver. Each time you add a clip, put the diver in the glass until it sinks.

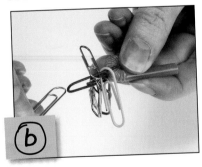

(b) When the diver finally sinks, remove one clip.

(c) The model diver should then float.

Sinking...

sinking...

sunk!

(1a)

Fill a large plastic drinks bottle with water. Add food colouring for fun. Drop in your model diver and screw the lid onto the bottle.

(1b)

Squeeze the middle of the bottle hard, then release your grip. If the diver does not dive and surface properly, remove it from the bottle and add or remove a paper clip.

(Q) **What happens to the diver?**

(A) **It sinks.** The straw is full of air and paper clips are needed to make it heavy enough to sink. When you squeeze the bottle, the air in the top of the bottle is squeezed into a smaller space. This increases the air pressure, which also increases the pressure inside the water. Water is squeezed into the straw, making it heavier, so the diver sinks. When the pressure is released, the air expands again. The water in the straw is forced out, making the diver lighter, and the straw surfaces.

49

Light and Sound

What is LIGHT?

Light is a type of energy that you can see and it is essential for all kinds of things. We need light to grow food and to be able to see around us. In earlier times, people used fires, candles or oil for lighting. Now we make our own light with electricity or gas.

How light travels

Light travels in straight lines, called rays. Light rays change direction if they are reflected off or pass through an object or substance, but they still remain straight.

Hot light

Light is usually produced by a very hot object, such as a fire, and heat is released. The Sun is our main source of light.

Cold light

Some animals produce light that gives off no heat. Fireflies are insects that can make parts of their body glow with light. About 1500 different deep-sea fish give off light.

Viperfish

Refraction

When a straw is placed in water, it looks as though it is slightly bent. This is because light rays bend when they pass through water. This bending of rays is called refraction.

Reflection

When light hits a very smooth surface such as a mirror, it reflects (bounces) off the surface. If it hits a mirror at an angle, it is reflected off at exactly the same angle.

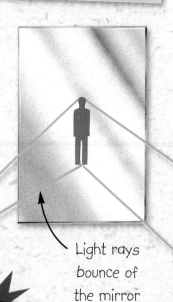

The eye receives a reflection of the image

Light rays bounce of the mirror

Actual object

What is SOUND?

Most sounds you hear, from the whisper of the wind to the roar of a jet, are actually moving air. Every sound originates with something vibrating. This makes the air vibrate too, and the vibrations in the air carry the sound to your ears. The vibrations that carry sound through the air are called sound waves.

Inside the ear

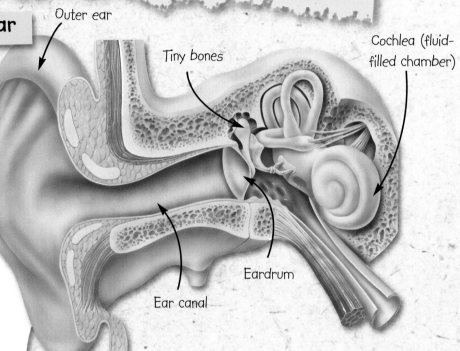

Outer ear

Tiny bones

Cochlea (fluid-filled chamber)

Eardrum

Ear canal

How do we hear sound?

The outer ear funnels sound waves into the ear. From there, sounds pass through a tube called the ear canal to the eardrum. Sounds make the eardrum and tiny bones in the middle ear vibrate. These bones pass the sound to the cochlea, in the inner ear, where nerve cells change the vibrations into messages that travel to the brain, which recognizes what we are hearing.

Sound measurement

The loudness (volume) of sound is measured in decibels (dB). A quiet sound, such as whispering, is 20 dB. A very loud sound, such as a jet plane taking off, is 120 dB.

Rustling leaves: 10 dB

Talking: 40 dB

Thunder: 100 dB

Atom bomb: 210 dB

Hand SHADOWS

Shadows are made when something blocks light. Try this experiment to make shadows that are big or small, sharp or blurred.

15 min | **No help needed** | **Easy**

You will need
- wall in a dark room
- torch or lamp

Preparation

Turn off all the lights and shut the curtains, so the room is as dark as possible. Shine the torch on a wall. Either hold it or rest it on a level surface.

1a

Point your finger upwards and hold it about 5 cm in front of the torch's light.

1b

Watch the shape of the shadow →

Move your hand another 5 cm away from the torch.

Q What does the shadow look like?

A It is large and blurred. Your hand is close to the light source, so it blocks out a wide area of the light beam, making a large shadow. Having a wide light source like a torch close to your hand makes the edges of the shadow blurred.

Move your hand about 20 cm away from the torch.

Then move your hand as far away from the torch and as close to the wall as you can (without touching the wall).

Q How does the shadow change?

A It becomes smaller and sharper. The further away your hand is from the light, the less of the beam your hand stops, so the smaller the shadow. The edges of the shadow are sharper because the light can't get round the edges of your hand.

Also try...

Put on a shadow puppet play. Make some puppets by cutting out card shapes, such as a horse or sheep. Then stick your puppet to a straw or short stick. Put these in front of the torch in the same way as you did with your hand. Start your 'On the Farm' play! Use these shapes to help you.

Ray of LIGHT

When you turn on a torch, it produces a ray of light. This experiment shows how light travels only in straight lines.

30 min | No help needed | Hard

You will need

- work surface
- thin A4 card (any colour)
- scissors
- modelling clay or sticky tack
- torch
- small mirror

Preparation

Make the slit about 2 mm wide

a

Carefully cut a piece of A4 card in half. Hold the pieces together and cut a slot 5 cm deep in one of the long edges.

b

Stand one of the pieces of card on its slotted edge. Support it with four pieces of sticky tack or modelling clay near the corners.

c

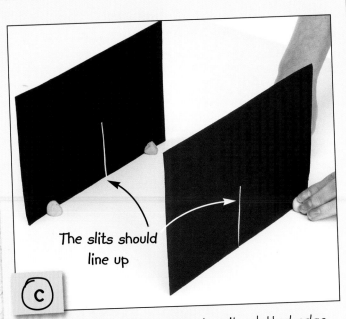

The slits should line up

Stand the other piece of card on its slotted edge, parallel to the first piece and about 15 cm away from it. Support it with four pieces of modelling clay. The slots in the cards should be roughly opposite each other.

1

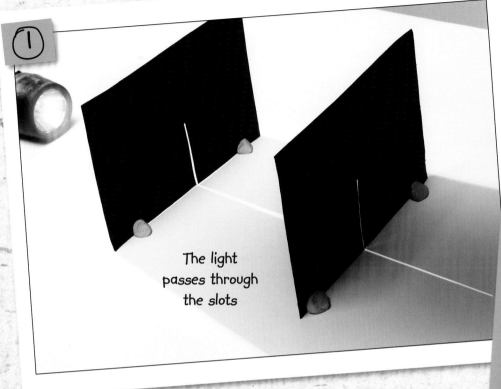

The light passes through the slots

Switch off the lights, or close the curtains to make the room dark. Shine a torch through one of the slots from about 10 cm away. Move the torch from side to side to make the ray pass through both slots.

Q What does the light do?

A The light ray passes through the slots. The light can only pass all the way through when the torch and both slots are all in line with each other. When the torch and slots are not in line, no light goes through the second slot. This shows that light travels only in straight lines.

2

Replace one piece of card with a mirror, with its reflecting side facing the remaining card. Shine the torch through the slot towards the mirror.

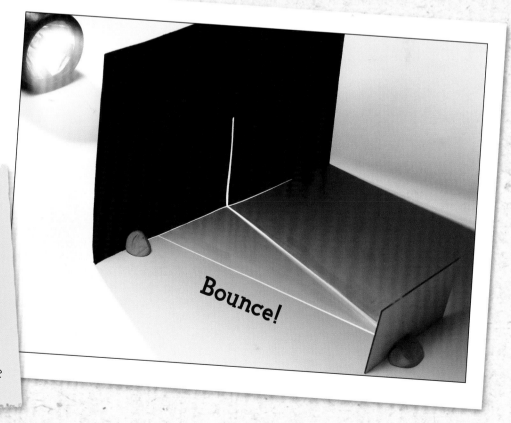

Bounce!

Q Does the light stop?

A No, the mirror reflects the light ray. The light ray that hits the mirror bounces back. When you move the torch from side to side, you'll see that the ray always bounces off the mirror at the same angle as it hits.

Through a LENS

In a camera, a glass or plastic lens bends light rays together to make an image that the camera records. Here's how to make a camera that makes a picture with just a simple hole.

30 min

Help needed

Hard

You will need

- work surface
- shoe box with lid
- scissors
- sticky tape
- tracing paper
- torch
- coloured card
- pin

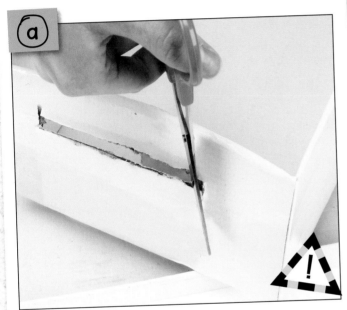

(a)

Carefully cut a hole about 8 cm by 5 cm in the centre of one side of the box.

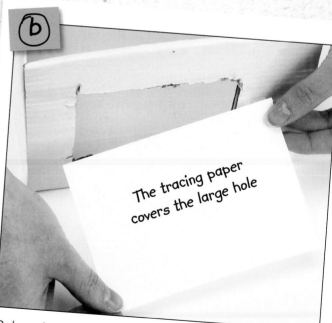

(b)

The tracing paper covers the large hole

Cut a piece of tracing paper about 10 cm by 7 cm. Stick it over the hole in the box, making sure it is not creased.

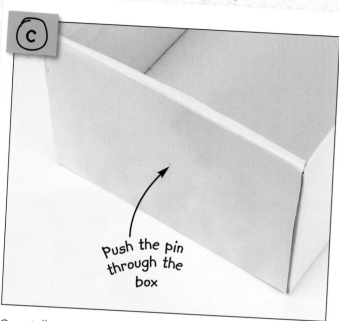

c

Push the pin through the box

Carefully push a pin through the box, opposite the first hole, to make a small, round hole.

e

Turn off any lights and make the room as dark as possible. Hold the box in front of your face with the tracing paper screen closest to you. Aim the box at the torch. If the image is dim, try draping a cloth over your head and the top of the box.

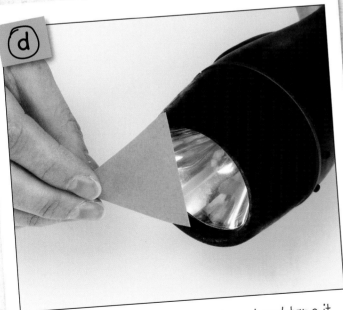

d

Cut a triangle shape in coloured card and tape it to the front of the torch. Turn on the torch and rest it at head height.

Q What can you see?

A An upside-down triangle! Rays of light coming from the torchlight go through the hole in the box and hit the screen. Light rays travel in straight lines, so rays travelling over the top of the triangle hit the bottom of the screen, and rays going under the bottom of the triangle hit the top of the screen.

Rainbow COLOURS

A rainbow is made when sunlight splits into different colours. Here's how to make these rainbow colours.

15 min · **Help needed** · **Hard**

You will need

- work surface
- dark room
- shallow plastic container
- water
- jug
- small mirror
- sticky tack
- white card
- torch

a Rest a small mirror in one end of the container, angled at about 45 degrees, with the reflecting side facing upwards. Add a small piece of sticky tack to hold the mirror in place.

Rest the card against a glass or pile of books

c Balance a piece of white card on the table at the other end of the plastic container.

b Half fill the plastic container with water.

d Make the room as dark as possible. Turn off the lights, close the curtains and block any light coming into the room.

The colours of the rainbow

The rainbow will appear on the card

e

Hold the torch about 10 cm away from the mirror and turn it on. Make sure you shine the light on the mirror underneath the water. Adjust the angle of the torch until you see the colours of the rainbow on the card. What can you see?

Also try... On a sunny day, stand with your back to the Sun and spray water into the air in front of you. The sunlight is split into colours as it enters and exits the tiny drops of water in the air, making a rainbow.

Q Why can you see a rainbow?

A Light from a torch and light from the Sun is called white light. It is made up of many different colours mixed together. The rays of light from the torch go into the water, bounce off the mirror, come out of the water again and hit the card. As the rays go in and out of the water they bend. The different colours bend by slightly different amounts, so they split up and you can see them. These colours are called the colours of the spectrum.

CHANGING colours

In these experiments, you can see how your eyes add colours, and how filters block out colours.

30 min   No help needed   Hard

You will need

- work surface
- white card
- small plate
- short pencil
- scissors
- water
- magneta (dark pink), cyan (blue/green) and yellow coloured pencils
- 3 clean, empty jars
- red, green and blue food colouring

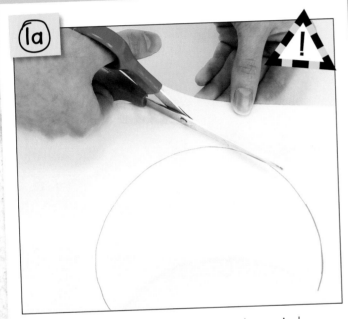

(1a)

Draw around the small plate to make a circle on the card. Carefully cut out the circle.

(1b)

Make your colours strong

Draw lines to divide the card into three equal sections. Colour the sections magneta, cyan and yellow.

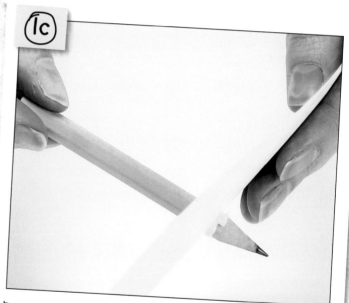

(1c)

Push a short, sharp pencil through the centre of the coloured circle. Stand the pencil on its tip on a hard surface and then spin it.

(Q) Which colour can you see?

(A) **When you spin the spinner, your eyes merge the colours to make white or grey.** By mixing cyan, magenta and yellow paints or coloured pencils in different amounts, you can make any colour you like. These special colours are called the primary colours of pigments.

Q Which two colours block light?

A Any two of red, green and blue. These are the primary colours of light. The jars are filters. Each one lets through only one colour of light (e.g. the red jar lets through only red light, and blocks green and blue). With two jars together, the colour that goes through the first is blocked by the second (so green light from the green jar is blocked by the red jar).

2a

Fill three jars with water. Add several drops of food colouring to each jar (red in one jar, blue in another jar and green in the last jar).

2b Stand the green jar in front of the other two jars, with a window or other light source behind them. Look through the green jar. What do you see? Then try standing the red and blue jars in front.

Only green can be seen

Only red comes ahead

Only blue shows through

Picture flicker BOOK

Here's how to make an optical toy that shows how our eyes are fooled into seeing movement on a television or cinema screen.

You will need

- work surface
- 12 or more small pieces of thin, white paper, about 10 cm by 8 cm
- stapler
- coloured pens or pencils

a

Trace each image carefully

Draw a clock face on each of the pieces of paper. It must be in exactly the same place and look exactly the same, so trace each one.

b

Draw the hands on each clock face

On each piece of paper, change the time by one hour. You should have 12 o'clock, 1 o'clock, 2 o'clock, 3 o'clock, and so on.

c

The time should start at
12 o'clock and then
count on, hour by hour

Staple the pieces of paper together, making sure they are in the right order.

Also try... Try drawing more difficult images with more than 12 pieces of paper.

d

Now flick the pages from start to finish whilst watching the clock faces.

Q What makes the image appear to be moving?

A The pictures on the pages pass in front of your eyes one after the other, in quick succession, each for a split second. Your brain remembers each image for a short time, so you get the impression of a moving clock hand. Television and films work in the same way, showing images in quick succession on the screen.

Seeing SOUND

You can't actually see sound as it travels through the air. But here's an experiment that lets you see the vibrations that sound is made from.

15 min No help needed Easy

You will need

- work surface
- balloon
- scissors
- glass or jar with a small opening
- sticky tape
- sugar or salt

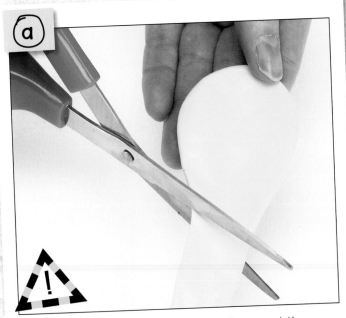

(a)

Carefully cut off the neck of a balloon and throw it away.

(b) Your glass should have a small opening to fit the balloon over

Put the body of the balloon over the top of a glass. Stretch it to make a tight skin, like that on a drum.

Wrap some sticky tape around the outside of the glass to keep the edge of the balloon in place.

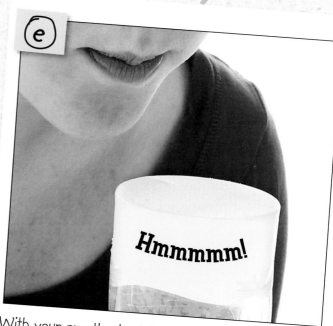

Hmmmmm!

With your mouth about 10 cm from the balloon's surface, hum loudly. Also try humming a high note and a low note.

Stand the glass on a table and put a few grains of salt or sugar on the balloon skin.

Q Do the grains on the balloon move?

A Yes! Sound is made up of vibrations that move through the air. The vibrations are called sound waves. When something makes a sound, vibrations spread out from it into the air in all directions. When the vibrations in the air hit something they make it vibrate, too. When sound waves from your mouth hit the stretched balloon, they make it vibrate up and down, which you can see because the grains jump up and down.

LIGHT
races sound

You hear sounds as soon as they are made. That's because sound travels really fast. Here's an experiment to prove it.

15 min   Help needed   Easy

You will need
- large outside space
- balloon
- flour
- funnel
- teaspoon
- pin
- helper

a Put the neck of a balloon over the funnel.

b Add the flour one spoonful at a time

Add a few spoonfuls of flour into the funnel and shake it down into the balloon.

c Remove the funnel, inflate the balloon and tie the neck to stop the air and flour from escaping. Don't inhale when blowing up the balloon – you'll get flour in your mouth.

d

Go outside to your large open space. Your helper should hold the balloon and a pin. Walk 100 large paces away from them.

Q Which comes first, hearing the balloon pop or seeing the flour explode?

A You should have seen the balloon burst, just before you heard the bang. This shows that light travels faster than sound. Light won the race easily. In fact, the difference in speeds is huge. Light travels at a staggering 300,000,000 metres a second – so fast that you see the balloon burst as it happens. Sound travels at just 340 metres a second. Its journey from the balloon will have taken just over half a second.

e

Ask your helper to hold the balloon away from their body. Look at the balloon and signal for your helper to pop it. Watch and listen very carefully – you will hear the balloon pop and see the flour escape.

Bang!

Musical BOX

The guitar and violin are both string instruments. Here's an experiment to see how strings make musical notes.

15 min   Help needed   Easy

You will need

- work surface
- shoe box with lid
- scissors
- 2 pencils or pens, the same thickness
- thick pen
- large elastic bands

Preparation

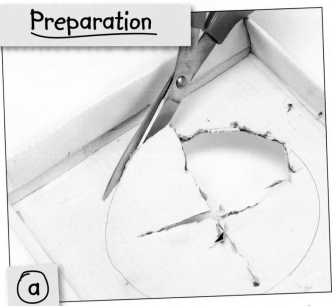

a Cut a round hole about 15 cm across at one end of the box lid. Put the lid back on the box.

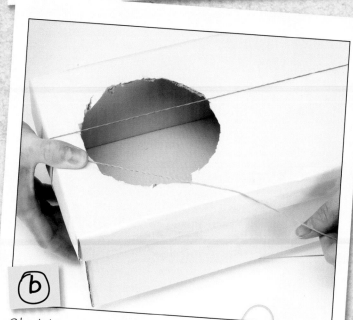

b Stretch a few elastic bands lengthways around the box so that they run across the centre of the hole.

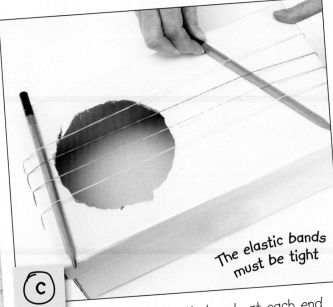

The elastic bands must be tight

c Put a pencil under the elastic bands at each end of the box. The pencils should lift the elastic bands clear of the hole.

Ping! Ping!

Pluck the elastic bands to make sounds. Pluck the bands hard to make loud sounds and softly to make quieter sounds.

Q Can you make sound?

A Yes because the elastic bands act as the string would on a guitar. When you pluck them, they vibrate from side to side. This vibrates the air around the strings, and you hear the vibrations as sound. The harder you pluck the strings, the stronger the vibrations are. Stronger vibrations make stronger sound waves, which sound louder. The box helps to make the sound louder because the sound bounces around inside it.

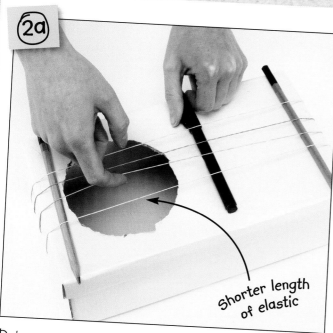

Shorter length of elastic

Put a pen thicker than the pencils under the bands close to the hole. Pluck the bands again.

2b

Try moving the pen backwards and forwards to play different notes.

Q Does the sound get higher?

A Yes, because the pen changes the length of the elastic bands that can vibrate freely. The shorter this is, the faster the bands vibrate, and the higher the notes they make.

BLOW some music

The clarinet, the trumpet and the recorder are all instruments you blow to move the air and make a sound. Try this experiment to see how these wind instruments work.

15 min | No help needed | Easy

You will need

- work surface
- square of card, 10 cm by 10 cm
- double-sided sticky tape
- 20 drinking straws
- scissors

a

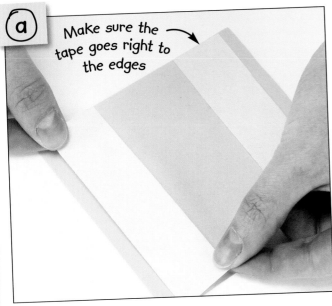

Make sure the tape goes right to the edges

Put two strips of double-sided sticky tape across the piece of card at opposite edges. Remove the backing.

b

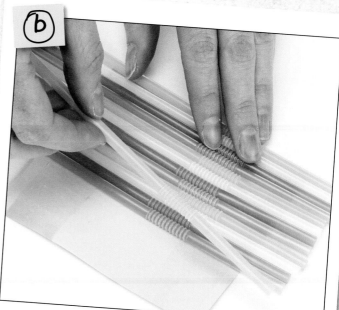

With the tape at the top and bottom, press the straws onto the tape side by side. The ends of the straws must line up along the top of the card.

(c)

Make sure the cut
ends open up

Diagonally cut off the bottoms of the straws. Cut across so that the first straw is about 10 cm long and the last straw is full length.

(d)

Hold the straw instrument with the tops of the straws near your bottom lip. Blow across the tops to produce sound.

Q What sounds do you make?

A **The short straws produce higher notes than the long straws.** The straws work as tubes. When you blow across the top, the moving air creates vibrations that travel up and down each straw. The harder you blow, the stronger the vibrations grow, so the louder the sounds become. The short straws produce higher notes because the speed of the vibrations depends on the length of the tube – smaller tubes create faster vibrations.

Also try...

Fill glass bottles with different amounts of coloured water. Blow across the tops of the bottles and listen to the different sounds you can make.

Matter and Materials

What is MATTER?

Matter makes up everything you can see, such as the chair you are sitting on. It also makes up the things you cannot see, such as the air you breathe. There are three states of matter, which make up nearly every substance in the Universe.

The three states of matter

Everything around us is either a solid, liquid or gas, made up of billions of units called atoms. Atoms are some of the smallest objects that exist, and are invisible.

A molecule is two or more atoms joined together.

A substance is groups of molecules.

Solid

Atoms or molecules in a solid cannot move. They are tightly packed together, so they keep their shape and feel firm.

If a solid is heated, it turns into a liquid. This is called melting.

If a liquid is cooled, it turns into a solid. This is called freezing.

Liquid

In a liquid, atoms or molecules can move or flow, but they stay the same distance apart. The links between the molecules are weaker than in a solid. A liquid can flow and fill the shape of its container.

If a gas is cooled, it turns into a liquid. This is called condensing.

If a liquid is heated, it turns into a gas. This is called evaporation.

Gas

Atoms or molecules in a gas move quickly and in all directions. The molecules bounce around because the forces between them are not strong enough to keep them together.

What are MATERIALS?

Every *substance* is made from a material, or a combination of materials. A material's properties, such as strength or flexibility (bendiness), make it useful for different things. Modern materials can be natural, or synthetic (chemically man-made).

Natural resources

Since ancient times, a large number of everyday materials have been made from plants, such as cotton and wood. Natural materials such as these need to be recycled (made into new things) and re-used, so they do not run out.

Wood

There are many different types of wood, varying in strength, colour, and weight. Wood comes from trees and is mainly used for fuel, or in construction (building).

Chair

Elastic bands

Rubber

Natural rubber is made from milky sap, called latex, found in some tropical trees. However, it can also be made synthetically. Rubber is flexible, tough and waterproof, which makes it useful for making car tyres.

Synthetic substances

Plastic, steel and glass are examples of synthetic materials. Sometimes a mixture of both natural and synthetic materials can be used – for example in clothing.

Drinks bottle

Plastic

Waterproof, long-lasting and strong, this synthetic material is mainly made from substances found in petroleum (crude oil). Plastics can be easily shaped and moulded and so are used in many everyday products.

Rope

Polyester

This synthetic material is often used to make clothing, as it dries quickly and holds its shape well. Rope is also often made from polyester because it is very strong.

ICE TO
water to steam

Ice, liquid water and steam are just water, but in solid, liquid and gas forms. Solids, liquids and gases are the three states of matter. This experiment shows that water has different properties in each of the three states.

15 min | Help needed | Easy

You will need

- hob
- saucepan with lid
- wooden spoon
- ice cubes
- thermometer that measures from 0°C to 100°C

Gently heat the saucepan and stir the ice. Ask an adult to help you heat the water on the hob because it will become hot. When the ice has begun to melt, test the temperature of the water with the thermometer.

Put a saucepan on the hob and cover the bottom of the saucepan with ice cubes. Press on the ice cubes with the wooden spoon and watch what happens.

Q Does the ice flow?

A No, at first the solid ice doesn't flow or change shape. As the temperature of the water rises, it changes state – from solid ice to liquid water. This change from solid to liquid is called melting, and for ice, it normally happens at 0°C.

Keep heating and melting the ice until you have liquid water. Look at how the liquid is different to the solid.

Extreme steam!

Soon you will see bubbles forming – the liquid water is turning to steam. Put a lid on the pan and turn off the heat before all the water is gone. You should have a pan full of steam. Don't touch the pan as the steam will be very hot.

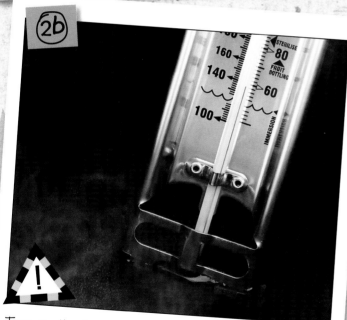

Turn up the heat. Ask an adult to help you test the temperature again to see if it has changed.

Q Does the water flow?

A Yes, the liquid water flows. It changes shape and flows to fill the bottom of the saucepan.

Q What does the steam do?

A The steam fills the saucepan. If you were to remove the lid, it would escape. The liquid water has changed to steam. This change of state is called boiling. For water, it normally happens at 100°C.

CREATE
crystals

Have you ever looked really closely at table salt or sugar? If so, you've already seen crystals. Here's how to grow some crystals of your own.

15 min preparation 3 days for results

Help needed

Hard

You will need

- work surface
- oven
- fridge
- table salt
- Epsom salts
- 2 glasses

- jug
- 2 teaspoons
- 4 saucers
- water
- optional: food colouring

Preparation

Half fill two glasses with warm water. Add a few teaspoons of table salt to one glass and a few teaspoons of Epsom salts to the other glass. Stir the water in each glass so that the salts dissolve. These are your salt solutions. You could add a few drops of food colouring for fun.

1a

Don't add too much solution to the water

Pour a little table salt solution onto two saucers. Leave one saucer in a warm place. Examine the crystals after one hour, then at regular intervals for about three days.

1b

Ask an adult to put the other saucer in the oven at 140°C/275°F/GM 1 for about 15 minutes or until all the water has evaporated. Carefully remove the crystals from the oven and examine them.

Q What shape are the crystals?

A The table salt crystals look like cubes. They are called cubic crystals. In the solution you made, the tiny particles of table salt were mixed with water. As the water evaporated in the air or oven, the particles joined together to make crystals. Crystals have straight edges and flat faces because the particles are arranged in a neat, regular way.

Crystals formed in the oven

After 15 minutes

Crystals formed in a warm place

After 3 days

2a Pour some Epsom salt solution onto two saucers. Put one saucer in a warm place and examine the crystals at regular intervals for a few days.

2b Put the other saucer in the fridge. Examine the crystals after 10 minutes, 30 minutes and one hour.

Q Are the Epsom salt crystals different?

A Yes, the Epsom salt crystals are needle shaped. Just like the cubic crystals, they have straight edges and flat faces.

After 3 days

Crystals formed in a warm place

Crystals formed in the fridge

After 1 hour

Mixing like MAGIC

Materials are made of millions of tiny particles. This experiment shows that in a liquid, the particles are constantly jiggling and moving.

15 min preparation 30 min for results	Help needed	Tricky

You will need

- work surface
- petroleum jelly
- 2 clean, empty jars
- food colouring
- water
- spoon
- jug
- piece of thin card
- washing-up bowl

(a) Smear plenty of petroleum jelly around the rims of the two jars to make a watertight seal.

Make the jelly really thick

(c) Fill the other jar with water, right to the top, too.

(b) Half fill one of the jars with water, add a few drops of food colouring and stir. Then fill the jar with water, right to the brim.

(d) Cut a square of thin card, large enough to cover the opening of one of the jars. Put the card on top of the jar with coloured water in it.

Make the card 2 cm bigger than the jar

e

The openings of the jars need to line up so the water doesn't leak out

Place the jar of clear water in a washing-up bowl. With one hand supporting the card, carefully turn over the jar of coloured water. Slowly slip out your hand and place the top jar on the bottom jar. You might need some help with this. Leave the jars to settle for 10 minutes before moving on to step f.

f

While holding the top jar steady, slowly and carefully slide out the card. Again, you might need some help with this step.

Dark red...

Clear...

After 1 minute

lighter...

darker...

After 10 minutes

light red!

light red!

After 30 minutes

Q What happens to the coloured water?

A It mixes with the clear water. The tiny water molecules are tightly packed together and are constantly moving. The water molecules from the two jars slowly mix together, carrying the particles of food colouring with them.

Can you MIX IT?

Many materials are made by mixing other materials. In these experiments, you'll put two different materials in the same container to see that some mix well and others don't mix at all.

15 min | No help needed | Easy

You will need
- work surface
- 5 jars
- cooking oil
- water
- 5 spoons
- table salt
- flour

①

Put some water and cooking oil into a jar and stir with a spoon.

②

Add salt or sugar

Half fill a clean jar with water, add a spoonful of salt and stir.

Q Do oil and water mix?

A No matter how much you stir, the oil and water don't mix. After stirring, they quickly separate again, leaving a layer of oil on top of the water. This is because the particles of oil and the particles of water repel each other.

Q Do salt and water mix?

A Yes, when you mix salt with water, the salt seems to disappear. In fact, it dissolves – it breaks into tiny particles that mix with the water. The mixture is called a solution.

3

Use a clean jar and mix a spoonful of flour into half a jar of water.

Q Do flour and water mix?

A Yes, flour and water mix. Unlike oil and water, flour mixes much better and forms a paste. This is because the water and flour do not repel each other.

Goooey!

5

Add as much salt as possible

Half fill a clean jar with water, add five spoonfuls of salt and stir. Add another five spoonfuls and keep stirring.

4

Pour some cooking oil into a clean jar. Add a few pinches of salt to the oil and stir.

Q How much salt will dissolve?

A Lots! Eventually you will not be able to make any more salt disappear into the water. There are no water particles free to break up any more salt.

Leftover salt

Q Do oil and salt mix?

A No, the salt does not dissolve. Instead it just sinks to the bottom. This is because the oil does not break up the salt crystals like water does.

SPLITTING the mix

A mixture is made up of two or more different materials mixed together. Sometimes you may want to separate the materials in a mixture.

30 min   No help needed   Hard

You will need

- work surface
- 3 clean, empty jars
- water
- teaspoon
- tea bag
- table salt
- peas (frozen or fresh, not tinned)
- colander
- washing-up bowl
- kitchen towel or filter paper

Preparation

Half fill three jars with water. Add some frozen or fresh peas to the first jar. Add the tea leaves from a tea bag to the second jar. Stir two teaspoons of salt into the third jar.

① Place a colander over a washing-up bowl. Pour half the mixture of water and peas into the colander.

Q Can you separate the peas?

A Yes, you can. The colander's holes are small enough to trap the peas.

Pour half the mixture of tea leaves and water through the colander, and then half the mixture of salt and water.

Q Can you separate tea or salt?
A No, they both stay with the water. The colander's holes are too large to trap tea leaves or salt particles.

Put a piece of kitchen towel in the colander. Pour the rest of the the tea and water mixture through.

Use clean kitchen towel

Put a new piece of kitchen towel in the colander. Pour the rest of the salt and water mixture through the paper. Dip your finger in the water and taste it.

Q Does a filter stop the tea leaves?
A Yes, it does. The kitchen towel has very small holes between the paper fibres. They are small enough to trap the tea leaves, but not the water.

Q Can you filter salt from water?
A No, the filter paper lets salt water through. This is why the water tastes salty. The particles of salt water are extremely tiny and easily pass through the holes.

83

SALTY to fresh water

Can you separate the salt and water in salty water? Yes, by distillation – try this experiment to see how.

30 min   Help needed   Tricky

You will need

- work surface
- hob
- water
- glass
- table salt
- teaspoon
- small dish
- saucepan
- kitchen foil
- ice cubes
- jug

a Half fill a glass with water. Add four teaspoons of salt and stir to make the salt dissolve. This is the salty solution.

b There should be no water in this dish

Pour most of the salty water into a saucepan. Then stand a small dish in the centre.

c Put a piece of kitchen foil over the top of the pan. Gently press down the centre of the foil slightly to make a dip. Put a few ice cubes in the dip.

84

d

Put the pan on the hob and heat it very gently. Allow the water to boil for a few minutes (but make sure all the solution does not boil away). Be careful as the water will get hot.

e

Make sure the dish is cold before you touch it

Remove the saucepan from the hob and leave it for one hour to cool completely. Then remove the foil. There should now be water in the dish. Taste the water in the pan and the water in the dish.

Q Do the waters taste different?

A Yes, the water in the dish is fresh water – free of salt. The water evaporated (turned to steam), leaving the salt behind in the pan, but the steam condensed (turned to water) on the cold foil and the water dripped into the dish. This process is called distillation and it is used to get fresh water from sea water.

Also try...

In the experiment on distillation, you removed the salt from the water and kept the water.

If you just want to keep the salt, put a saucer of the salty water in a warm place. The water will slowly evaporate, leaving the salt behind.

COLOUR separation

Inks, food colouring and dyes are often mixtures containing different colours called pigments. Try this experiment to separate pigments so that you can see what they are.

30 min   No help needed   Hard

You will need

- work surface
- 4 strips of filter paper, 2 cm by 10 cm
- water
- 4 clean, empty jars
- 4 pencils or short sticks
- sticky tape
- 4 water-soluble felt-tip pens or food colouring
- scissors
- water
- jug

(a)

Wrap a strip of filter paper around each of your four pencils, so the paper is as long as your jar is tall. Stick it to the pencil with sticky tape.

Trim any excess paper

(b)

Put about 2 cm of water in each of the four jars.

(c)

Use plenty of food colouring or ink

About 2 cm from the end of each strip, either draw a large dot with a felt-tip pen or add a drop of food colouring.

(d)

Carefully lower a strip (with the coloured dot at the bottom end) into each jar, so the dot is about one centimetre above the water's surface. Examine the paper every ten minutes for an hour.

(Q) What happens to the dots?

(A) **The colours spread out and separate.**
The filter paper strips soak up the water. The water picks up the different pigments in the ink and carries them upwards through the paper. The water on the paper slowly evaporates, and this draws more water upwards. Different pigments are carried different distances up the paper, and so are separated.

After 10 minutes

green = yellow + blue

After 30 minutes

yellow – no change

blue = red + blue

red = yellow + purple

After 60 minutes

87

CABBAGE colours

What links lemon juice and bleach? One is an acid and the other is an alkali. They are opposites. Here's an experiment to show what is acid and what is alkali – using cabbage!

30 min   Help needed   Tricky

Preparation

(a) Ask an adult to chop half a red cabbage into small pieces.

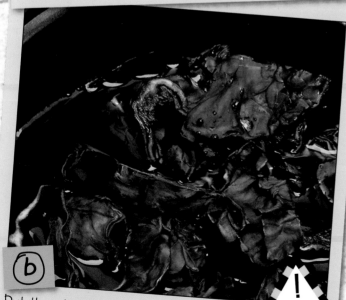

(b) Put the pieces of cabbage in a saucepan and cover with water. Ask an adult to bring it to the boil and simmer for five minutes. Turn off the heat and allow the water and cabbage to cool.

(c) Hold a sieve over the washing-up bowl. Pour the cabbage and water through it, so the purple water collects in the bowl.

(d) Half fill the three jars with some of the purple water. The purple colour means the liquid is neutral.

1

Jar 1

Add a few drops of bleach to the first jar and stir. Ask an adult to help you pour the bleach.

Q What does bleach do to the water?

A It turns the purple water green, then yellow. Bleach is an alkali.

2

Jar 2

Put a few drops of lemon juice into the second jar and stir.

Q What does lemon juice do to the water?

A Lemon juice turns the water red. It is an acid.

3

Jar 3

Put a teaspoon of bicarbonate of soda into the third jar and stir.

Q What does bicarbonate of soda do to the water?

A It turns the purple colour to blue. Bicarbonate of soda is a chemical called a base, which turns water into an alkali. But it is not as alkaline as the bleach.

Bleach

Strong alkali

Lemon

Acid

Bicarbonate of soda

Weak alkali

By changing colour, the cabbage water tells us whether chemicals are acids or alkalis. It is called an indicator.

Bubbles AND FROTH

A chemical reaction is where materials are changed into new materials. Here's your chance to see chemical reactions at work.

You will need

- work surface
- milk
- 2 glasses
- tablespoons
- vinegar
- filter paper
- funnel
- bicarbonate of soda
- small plastic drinks bottle
- balloon
- saucer

1a

Put half a cup of milk into a glass and stir in two tablespoons of vinegar. The vinegar will make the milk turn lumpy.

1b

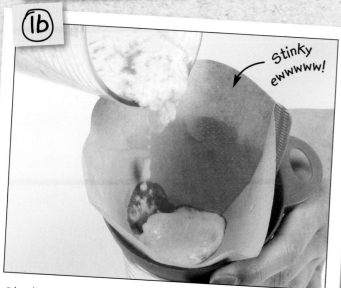

Stinky ewwwww!

Strain the mixture through filter paper into another glass. You don't need to keep the liquid.

1c

After an hour or two, remove the pasty substance from the paper onto a saucer.

Q What do vinegar and milk make?

A They make a pasty substance. A material called casein in the milk reacts with the vinegar to make a new substance, which goes hard like plastic when it dries.

Touch it, if you dare!

②a

Put the narrow part of a funnel into the neck of a balloon. Carefully put two tablespoons of bicarbonate of soda into the funnel and shake it down into the balloon.

Up, up and away!

②b

Don't tip any bicarbonate of soda into the bottle yet

Add 2 cm of vinegar to the bottle. Then carefully attach the balloon to the top of the bottle.

②c

Lift up the balloon and shake it so the bicarbonate of soda falls into the bottle.

Q What happens to the balloon?

A The balloon inflates! The vinegar reacts with the bicarbonate of soda, making carbon dioxide gas. This gas fills the balloon.

ELECTRIC bubble-maker

In this experiment you send electricity through water. The electricity breaks up the water, making tiny bubbles of gas.

30 min

No help needed

Hard

You will need

- work surface
- thick card
- clean, empty jar
- 2 lead pencils, the same length
- pencil sharpener
- water
- 9V battery

(a) Cut a square of thick card about 2 cm wider than the opening of the jar.

(b) Sharpen both ends of the pencils. Then carefully push the pencils through the card, about 2 cm apart.

(c) Don't let the pencils touch the bottom

Half fill the jar with water. Then place the card on top of the jar and slide the pencils up or down so that their ends are level and underwater.

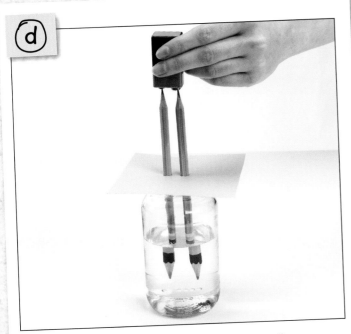

(d)

Hold the battery upside down on top of the pencils so that the battery terminals touch the pencil leads.

Also try...

Add some salt to the water, stir it in and repeat the experiment. Sniff the air above the jar.

Can you smell chlorine or a 'swimming pool' smell? When you add salt, chlorine comes from the pencil lead attached to the positive terminal. Chlorine is one of the elements in salt (which is sodium chloride, or NaCl).

pop!
pop!
pop!

bubbly

(Q) **Can you see bubbles?**

(A) **The small bubbles that appear on the pencil leads and rise to the surface are bubbles of oxygen and hydrogen.** These are the two chemical elements in water. Oxygen is produced when the pencil lead touches the positive battery terminal, and hydrogen is made when the pencil lead touches the negative battery terminal.

GLOSSARY

Acid A chemical substance that has a pH level of less than 7.

Air pressure The force exerted by the weight of tiny particles of air.

Air resistance The push of air against a moving object.

Alkali A chemical substance that has a pH level of more than 7.

Angle The space between two straight lines or surfaces that join each other, usually measured in degrees.

Atom The smallest particle of an element.

Bernoulli's principle The theory that high-speed air has lower pressure than still air.

Boiling point The temperature at which a liquid bubbles and changes into a gas when it is heated.

Buoyancy When an object is able to float.

Charge A property that causes particles to attract or repel each other. Objects can have either a positive or negative charge.

Circuit A loop through which electricity can flow.

Cold light A kind of light that gives off no heat.

Colours of the spectrum The rainbow colours you see when white light is broken up.

Condensing The process of a gas changing to a liquid as it cools.

Conductor A material, such as copper, which allows the flow of an electrical current.

Decibel (dB) A unit for measuring the loudness (volume) of sound.

Detector A device that recognizes the presence of electricity in a circuit.

Dissolving If a solid dissolves, it mixes with a liquid and makes a solution.

Distillation The process used to separate a liquid from a solution by evaporation and condensing.

Drag Also known as air resistance.

Electromagnet A strong magnet that is only magnetic when an electric current passes through it.

Element A simple chemical substance that consists of only one kind of atom, and can not be broken down.

Evaporation The process by which molecules change from liquid to gas when heated.

Expanding To become or make larger.

Floating An object will float on water if the upthrust is equal to or greater than the object's weight.

Freezing point The temperature at which a liquid cools and changes into a solid.

Hot light The light that is produced by a very hot object, such as the Sun. Heat is also released.

Inflate To fill a balloon, or other expandable object, with air or gas so that it becomes bigger.

Insulator A material, such as rubber, that does not conduct electricity.

Magnetic field The area around a magnet inside which its magnetic force can be detected. An electric current creates a magnetic field.

Material What every substance is made from. Materials can be natural (e.g. wood), or synthetic (e.g. polyester).

Matter All substances are made up of very small

particles, or matter, and can be a solid, liquid or gas.

Melting The process that changes a solid into a liquid, mainly when heated.

Mixture A substance that contains two or more different substances that are mixed, but not chemically bound. They can be easily separated.

Molecule At least two atoms held together by a chemical bond.

Negative charge When a substance is negatively charged, it gains electrons.

Neutral A chemical substance with a pH level equal to 7.

Nitrogen The gas that makes up the majority of air (78 percent).

Optical Relating to machines or processes to do with light, images or the way we see things.

Oxygen An essential gas to all living things. It makes up 21 percent of air.

Parallel circuit A circuit where an equal amount of electricity flows through two objects, such as light bulbs, at the same time.

pH scale The measure of how acidic or alkaline a solution is.

Pigment A mixture of different colours that make up one colour when put together.

Positive charge When a substance becomes positively charged, it loses electrons.

Re-using Using materials again in their original form rather than throwing them away.

Reaction When a chemical change occurs and materials are changed into new materials. E.g. when vinegar reacts with bicarbonate of soda, carbon dioxide is made.

Recycling When materials are taken to a plant where they can be melted and re-made into either the same or new products.

Reflection When light hits a very smooth surface and bounces off it.

Refraction The bending of light rays when they pass through a substance, such as water.

Separation When two or more materials in a mixture are moved apart.

Series circuit A circuit where electricity flows through one object, such as a light bulb, and then straight on to another object.

Sinking An object will sink if its weight is greater than the upthrust of the water.

Solution A mixture in which a gas, solid or liquid is dissolved in a liquid.

Sound waves The vibrations in the air that carry sound to your ears.

Streamlined An object that is shaped to move smoothly and easily, with little resistance, through air or water.

Surface tension Water molecules at the surface are pulled towards each other, and so act like a skin.

Thermometer A piece of equipment used to measure temperature.

Vibrate To move, or cause to move, a short distance quickly and continuously.

Water pressure The push of water caused by its weight. The deeper the water, the higher the pressure.

White light Light that is made up of many different colours mixed together, such as light from the Sun.

Notes for HELPERS

Help and hazards

Help needed

- All of the experiments are suitable for children to conduct, but they will need help and supervision with some. This is usually because the experiment requires the use of sharp equipment. These experiments are marked with a 'Help needed' symbol.

- Read the instructions together before starting and help to assemble the equipment before supervising the experiment.

- It may be useful to carry out your own risk assessment to avoid any possible hazards before your child begins. Check that long hair and any loose clothing are tied back.

- Be careful when handling wire strippers, scissors or knives, or lighting matches and using heat. Ensure that all equipment is tidied away safely after use.

Extra experiments

Also try...

You can also help your children with the extra experiments in this book, or search the Internet for more, similar ideas. There are hundreds of science experiment websites to choose from.

www.kids-science-experiments.com This website is packed with simple, fun experiments for your children to enjoy.

www.sciencebob.com/experiments/index.php Engaging science experiments with clearly explained instructions will keep your kids busy for hours.

www.tryscience.org You will find lots of entertaining and informative experiments on this colourful, interactive website.